A HISTORY OF COUNTY KILDARE

D1578896

A HISTORY OF COUNTY
Kildare

Padraic O'Farrell

GILL & MACMILLAN

To the good people of Staplestown with whom I grew up

Gill & Macmillan Ltd
Hume Avenue, Park West, Dublin 12
with associated companies throughout the world
www.gillmacmillan.ie

© Padraic O'Farrell 2003

0 7171 3462 8
Index compiled by Helen Litton
Design by Graham Thew Design
Print origination by Carrigboy Typesetting Services, Co. Cork
Printed by ColourBooks Ltd, Dublin

This book is typeset in 11pt Post-Mediaeval on 14pt.

The paper used in this book comes from the wood pulp of managed forests. For every tree felled, at least one tree is planted, thereby renewing natural resources.

A CIP catalogue record for this book is available from the British Library.

1 3 5 4 2

CONTENTS

NOTE 1: Irish counties or shires began emerging in the late twelfth century. The shiring process installed a sheriff whose authority included administration, military and legal functions. The shiring of Kildare in the thirteenth century was one of the last. To distinguish between Kildare town and county, however, the term Co. Kildare is used throughout this text.

NOTE 2: Every effort is made to include birth and death dates on first introduction of individuals. Due to the local nature of the work, however, this is not always possible.

# ACKNOWLEDGEMENTS

RETURNING TO MY PLACE OF BIRTH to write this book became a happy experience thanks to a number of people, many of whom were not born when I left. Mario Corrigan of Co. Kildare Library gave assistance far and above the call of duty. He welcomed me warmly and responded to every request for information with extraordinary enthusiasm and speed. He read the MSS and made suggestions. The Chief Executive of Co. Kildare Library and Arts Service (Riverbank), Michael Kavanagh, assisted me previously and he too read part of the MSS and commented. Responsibility for errors that may appear in the work remain my own, of course. Jim Mullally, Nuala Hartnett, Paula Behan and others of the library staff also helped greatly.

I joined Co. Kildare Fáilte Ltd. for a memory-refreshing and updating tour of the county. Then and later, Karen Gorey and Benita White were most helpful, Benita giving considerable assistance in acquiring illustrations.

I thank KELT; Croke Park Museum; Harry Lynch, Norman Black, Marie McCormack and Kathleen Murtagh at Midland-East Tourism headquarters; executives and staff of Westmeath Co. Library; the National Library of Ireland; Trinity College Library; and the National Archives.

At Saint Patrick's College, Maynooth, Rev. Ronan Drury, Editor of *The Furrow*, Penny Woods and Celia Kehoe of the Russell Library, Elizabeth Murphy and other members of the staff of Pope John Paul XXIII Library were all most helpful, as was Mary O'Malley of the college's visitors' centre.

Others who assisted greatly include Sean Haughey of the Oireachtas Library; Karen Seyman, Diocesan Secretary of Meath and Kildare; Margaret Doyle, Clongowes Wood College; Commandants Victor Laing and Pat Brennan at the Military Archives, Cathal Brugha Barracks, Dublin; Kildare Town Heritage Centre; Athy Heritage Centre; Gay Brabazon; Desmond Egan; Viv Abbott, Paddy Power and Brian Kelly (KELT).

Compute-IT, Mullingar, came to my rescue when a vicious virus struck. My daughters, Niamh and Aisling, again helped with word processing while my wife, Maureen, put her proof-reading skills to work once again.

I am most grateful to my publishers Gill & Macmillan, where, as usual, Fergal Tobin continues to encourage with warmth and wit and where Deirdre Rennison Kunz edits with patience and courtesy.

Padraic O'Farrell, 2003

I

In An
ACORNSHELL

The PRESENT COUNTY KILDARE (Cill Dara/Church of the Oak) is roughly triangular in shape with its apex to the south. It covers 169,386 hectares of the flattest terrain in Ireland. Only in the extreme east, where it rises to meet neighbouring Co. Wicklow and begins kneading foothills for that county's mountain range, does it exceed 305 metres above sea level. Cupidstown Hill near Kilteel is, at 380 metres, the county's highest point. The Hill of Allen with its tower on top and neighbouring Dunmurry in the Red Hills south-east of Rathangan are greater in legend and folklore than in elevation at 206 metres and 232 metres respectively. These are the most northerly of the inliers of older rocks (Lower Palaeozoic and Old Red Sandstone) in south-central Ireland, and they also contain volcanic basalt.

Besides Wicklow and Dublin to the east, Co. Kildare has boundaries with Meath to the north, Carlow to the south, and Offaly and Laois to the west. The source and initial flow of the River Boyne are to be found in the north and the county also accommodates stretches of the Liffey and Barrow and of the Royal and Grand Canals.

Forming a significant portion of the central limestone plain, Co. Kildare boasts the broad plains of the Curragh, once known as Cuireach Life, suggesting that the River Liffey then embraced it. The unique

Pollardstown Fen hides in the county's centre and a significant area of the Bog of Allen occupies the west and north-west of the county.

Close to the country's capital, Dublin, the modern Co. Kildare has a number of major industries and leisure facilities. It also contains prime farming land with fine beef-fattening pastures. There is some forestry and perhaps too much stone and gravel excavation. Ireland's largest military camp and many of its top horse-training and racing establishments are in and around the Curragh plain which on fine summer days becomes a gorse-scented picnicking playground for tired city folk. Villages and townlands that were once quiet, rural backwaters have become busy dormer-towns. The county's population rose by 21.5 per cent (134,992 to 163,995) between the census of 1996 and 2002. The most common surnames in the county today include Brennan, Byrne, Carey, Casey, Doyle, Dunne, Kavanagh, Kelly, Keogh, Lawlor, Moore, Murphy, Nolan, O'Connor, O'Neill, O'Farrell and O'Toole.

Naas is the county's administrative centre and the other main towns include Athy, Celbridge, Clane, Kilcock, Kildare, Leixlip, Monasterevin and Newbridge (Droichead Nua).

Co. Kildare once straddled the Pale (see Chapter 4) and traces of that boundary's ramparts are still visible near Clongowes Wood College, where James Joyce (1882–1941) was once a pupil.

Like their native terrain, Kildare people have little modulation in their accent. Solid and often easy-going, they do not boast about their county's considerable history, as evidenced by its wealth of antiquities. Their passions are more often focused on the progress of the 'Lilywhites', the county's Gaelic footballers, whom they revere almost as much as the county's racehorses.

ANTIQUITY: EARLIEST TIMES to FOURTH CENTURY AD

KELETONS FOUND IN Co. Waterford in 1928 indicated
that Final Palaeolithic hunters lived there during the Late Glacial
period, probably between 10000 BC and 8500 BC. With their
simple stone tools and weapons these hunters would have crossed a
land bridge from Scotland and as they reached Waterford, it is conceivable that they also discovered what later became Co. Kildare.

The animals they hunted with primitive weapons included bears,
Arctic foxes, lemmings and other rodents. The most prized prey was the
giant Irish deer, whose stag's heavy antlers often caused it to topple into
watering holes when drinking. Glaciation restricted its food supply,
however, and the species became extinct. Some of their antlers and
bones came to light in Rathcoffey, near Clane, in April 1945. Mesolithic
(Middle Stone Age c. 7500–4500 BC) hunting and fishing communities
were evolving after 6000 BC when Ireland was a forested island. Some
of these would have arrived in hide and timber boats from the Iberian
peninsula. These sea-faring explorers, apprehensive about facing the
Atlantic ocean, regarded Ireland as *Ultima Thule*, the 'back of beyond', or
final stop on their voyage. The laying of a gas pipe through Clane
during 1998–9 incorporated an archaeological study which unearthed a
Bann Flake,a Later Mesolithic instrument which would have been used
as a knife c. 4500 BC.

EARLY FARMING

Stock and crop farming communities began forming c. 4000 BC. They used sea lanes from England and France and trussed their stock in their fragile craft. Inward movement from coastal regions increased and Co. Kildare would have been an attractive area for settlers. Their presence at Dún Áilinne, near Kilcullen (see below) and at the Moat (motte) of Ardscull, near Athy, has been accepted. During the final Neolithic Period (New Stone Age, c. 5000 to 4000 BC in Atlantic Europe), farming instruments, pottery, domestic animals and agricultural techniques were becoming common. The laying of the Dublin-Cork gas line in the 1980s exposed a Neolithic flint blade and scraper at Moone.

BRONZE AGE

Complex burial chambers, passage graves and tombs were a feature of the Bronze Age which is believed to have reached Ireland c. 2400 BC. Some archaeologists consider these to have been community focal points or territorial markers and therefore of greater significance than mere burial places. They pre-dated the Egyptian Pyramids. Mullamast, near Ballitore may have been one, while Dún Áilinne was a ceremonial summit site with a rampart and internal ditch. Small sepulchral mounds were once obvious on the Curragh. Gallauns of note were situated at Mullamast, Punchestown, Harristown, Ballymore Eustace and Forenaughts (Furness). Near these, archaeologists have unearthed cremated bones, flint knives and potsherds (pottery shards). They may have been boundary marks or memorial stones but ritualistic or phallic connotations cannot be ruled out.

The ritual circular enclosure known as the Piper's Stones at Kilgowan, near Kilcullen, contains fourteen granite rocks and an outlier. They represent, respectively, dancers and a piper. Tradition holds that they were revellers who became petrified for violating the Sabbath.

Co. Kildare contains large tracts of fen and bogland which are the result of water holdings left by retreating ice of the second glacial period. The science of dendrochronology, which matches dates with rings formed annually in tree trunks, has shown that bog growth where the Co. Kildare-Offaly border nears Edenderry was greatest c. 3100 BC and 300 BC but was also significant c. 4900, 3600 and 2200 BC.

Expertise in metalwork during the Bronze Age led to the manufacture of more lethal weapons. Warring factions used them while pursuing their covetous instincts and forming rudimentary kingships. Kings had their court magicians then and a legend exists that one of them magically transported the 1700 BC Stonehenge formation on England's Salisbury Plain from the edge of the Curragh. In 1200, the Welsh chronicler Giraldus Cambrensis (c. 1147–1223), nephew of Maurice FitzGerald, Lord of Maynooth and Naas (see The Geraldines, Chapter 4), described the similarity of the Stonehenge stones and some found 'near Naas', while writing:

> In ancient times there was in Ireland a remarkable pile of stones called 'The Giant's Dance,' because the giants brought it from the farthest parts of Africa into Ireland and set it up . . . on the plains of Kildare near Naas . . . According to the 'British History' [Historia Britonum by Geoffrey de Monmouth] Aurelius Ambrosius, King of Britain, caused these stones to be transported from Ireland to Britain by the divine aid of Merlin . . .

Ring formations in bog oak studied by dendrochronologists found in the Bog of Allen and elsewhere suggest that a catastrophic climate change occurred in 1159 BC and lasted for eighteen years. This begot a territory in which there was little or no sunlight and in which superstitious people began sacrificing animals and humans to appease whatever deity they thought responsible for their plight. In that situation, fear would have spread across the land, making factions more aggressive. A more prosperous situation c. 800 BC led to the manufacture of sophisticated metalwork that produced ornate collars, costume ornamentation and bracelets.

RAVAGES AND RAMPARTS

The Greeks referred to barbarian races to their north as Keltoi. These Celts reached Ireland during the first century BC and began to establish their language (Gaelic) and culture here. Theories claiming a Celtic 'invasion' have been refuted, although there is an acceptance that some imposition on established communities took place c. 200 BC. Great roadways began linking important sites (see below). Communities assessed a man's wealth by the number of cattle he owned and a tax levied in cattle was called Bóramha (also Bórúma, Anglicised as Boru). The great literary epic of An Táin underlines the important place of the cow in commerce and in status.

From AD 111 to AD 119, during the reign of Felimy Reachtmar (Lawgiver), Munster invaders occupied Ossory and south Leinster territories. After numerous attempts to dislodge them they suffered a defeat at a ford on the River Greese near Mullamast, thereafter called Áth-Tristean, or 'the Ford of Conflict'. After retreating to the River Barrow they lost another fight at another ford where a prominent Munster chief called Aé lost his life, giving Athy its name (Áth Aé/Ford of Aé).

The King of Tara, Tuathal Teachtmar, married Darina, younger daughter of Eochy Aincheaun, King of Leinster. Later, Eochy locked Darina in his palace at Naas, went to Tara and proclaimed her dead. He asked for Tuathal's other daughter, Fithir, in lieu and the High King consented. Meanwhile, Darina had escaped and was wandering towards Tara when she met her husband and sister. Fithir died of fright and Darina of a broken heart. In revenge, Tuathal mustered his forces and ravaged Leinster. He subjected its citizens to a Bóramha, 6,000 each of cows, sheep, pigs, mantles and ounces of silver. He destroyed settlements on the sites of modern Naas and Allen and slaughtered their inhabitants.

Ramparts like Dún Aengus on the Aran Islands began appearing and since the Roman invasion of Britain did not reach Ireland, these may have been defences against robbers and pirates, or mere status symbols of their time. Burial sites and mounds began taking on a mythological connection. When communities considered that one of these allowed access to the Otherworld, they called it a sidh, or fairy mound.

Nuadha, a formidable Celtic god, was son of the goddess Danu and ruled the Tuatha Dé Danaan on two occasions. He features in the epic tale of the Battle of Moytura and his sword finds mention in Arthurian legend. Maynooth (Maigh Nuadha) means 'The Plain of Nuadha' and the Hill of Allen (Cnoc Almhan, formerly Almú) was the god's sidh. Legend tells how Fionn Mac Cumhaill received Allen from his grandfather Tadhg, Nuadha's son. The tradition of Fionn and the Fianna was foremost in the Gaelic regions of Scotland, Ireland and the Isle of Man. From the Celtic 'Vindos' the name Fionn has Viennese origins and its storytelling cycle ranks with Homer's *Odyssey* and *Iliad* and other

European epical traditions. Napoleon (1769–1821) and Thomas Jefferson (1743–1826) were said to have found inspiration in the corpus.

IRON AGE

In Europe, the Iron Age lasted from about the third century BC into the Christian period. The Age is reflected in Irish literary accounts of great battles, of kings and queens and handsome princes in chariots. Legends of a mystical Otherworld found a voice in oral tradition and the Hill of Allen became forever fixed as the seat of Fionn Mac Cumhaill and his followers. It was to that area of Kildare that Oisín returned from Tír na nÓg after 300 years and, heartbroken at the changes he observed, headed for Gleann na Smól (Valley of the Thrushes) in Dublin, where the Fianna once enjoyed recreation. There he leaned from his horse to help some men who were trying to move a large boulder. The stirrup broke, Oisín fell, and as soon as he touched the ground he became an old man. Despite the legendary aspect of the Fianna, the *Annals of the Four Masters* record that an enemy cast a javelin at Fionn and killed him at Áth-Brea (probably Áth Buí, Athboy) on the River Boyne in AD 283.

Earthen rings on the Hill of Carbury enclosed Iron Age cremations and inhumations. A late nineteenth century record notes that a rare kitchen containing metal instruments, including axes, arrow-heads and pins was enclosed in a pre-historic tuam at Kennycourt, Brannockstown.[1] In 1942 a set of tools was discovered at Bishopsland, Ballymore Eustace. Dated c. 1200 BC, it contained tools for metalwork, woodwork and harvesting. It may have belonged to a smith or other such tradesman.

ANCIENT BOUNDARIES

Ireland did not endure Roman conquest so the land divisions of the Gaelic society that existed at the close of the Iron Age have, to a considerable extent, survived in the barony system (see Medieval). A king, or rí, ruled each túath, or small hierarchical community. The king of the greatest tuath governed 'over-realms' of his own and lesser units.

There were five main federations of these 'over-realms': Uladh, Laighin, Mumhain, Connachta and Midhe (Ulster, Leinster, Munster, Connaught and Meath). While a High King ruled these from Tara, his effective power was minimal outside Leinster, Meath and Connaught.

The astronomer and mathematician Ptolemy (fl. AD 127–145) described Co. Kildare as being inhabited by the Coriundi, whose lands lay west of the rivers Liffey and Slaney. The Cauci and Menapii occupied the east, the Eblani were on the north, and the Brigantes on the south. The county formed part of the district of Galen, or Caellan, that is, most of the existing county and parts of Wicklow and Carlow. Galen was heavily forested, a fact borne out by the profusion of 'bog oak' or remains of trees found in Kildare's many bogs. Ptolemy noted that the native chieftains of the district were the heads of the family of Hy Caellan, or McKelly, whose principal residence was at Rath Ardscull, the Moat of Ardscull. Later, the area became known as Magh-Cloinne Ceallaigh (Plain of the O'Kelly sept). Ptolemy also marked an inland city of Rheba, since accepted as Rheban.

ROADWAYS

The Esker Riada, also known as the Via Magna or Sligh Mór, consisted of a series of great gravel ridges stretching from east to west, dividing Ireland into the Leath Chuinn and Leath Mogha. It was one of about five major slighthe (roads) serving Tara and was probably pre-historic. Although it passed through Kildare, its precise route is a subject of argument. It may have traversed the county's present border with Co. Meath. At a later period, however, Saint Patrick is said to have joined it at Dunmurraghill. This supports a theory that it ran through Celbridge, Taghadoe, Donadea, Staplestown, Timahoe and Mainistear Fheorais (Monasterosis or Bermingham's Monastery in Carbury where Sir John Birmingham founded a Franciscan friary in 1325).

The Slighe Dhála Meic Umhóir, or Bealach Muighe Dála, running southward passed through Oughterard north of Kill, Naas, Droichead Nua, the Curragh and Kildare town.

GEOLOGY

The Leinster granite range includes parts of Kildare. On its border lies Cambro-Silurian rock, unaltered portions of which are fossiliferous. The Chair of Kildare, north-west of the Curragh, is an isolated example. It protrudes upwards through Carboniferous rocks. Paroptesis, or change caused by dry heat, transformed some rocks into hornstone (baked slates or shale), and coloured grit. In common with other Leinster counties, Kildare has a three-fold division in limestones. Lowest of these are bedded limestones, some described by geologists as Lower Shaly. Above this division they lose their bedded character, adopting the Fenestella type between groups. Some Calp based limestones represent the Lower Carboniferous type. To the west and north of Maynooth there are traces of coal measures.

Mineral locations include Ardclough (lead), Carbury (lead), Celbridge (lead and zinc), Freagh and Punchersgrange (copper) and Upper Wheatfield (lead and zinc). The deposits at Freagh and Wheatfield were worked.

APPROACHING CHRISTIANITY

Tracing pre-Christian Kildare does not produce a conclusive result. Theories evolve from considerable conjecture based on scant evidence. Four centuries after Christ, the Roman Empire's influence was dissipating. *Scoti* was Roman for Irish, and Scotland, therefore, the Land of the Irish. Irish seafarers raided Scotland and the rest of Britain, often bringing back slaves. Schoolchildren from Kilcock to Athy and from Ballymore Eustace to Monasterevin ignore some dissenting historians and insist that Saint Patrick was one of these and that he came to Ireland around the year AD 432.

3 CHRISTIANITY

I T IS LIKELY THAT Christian bishops existed in Ireland before Saint Celestine I (Pope from 422–432) sent Palladius here c. 431. That he did so is conceivable because the Roman Empire officially adopted Christianity in 313 and the Irish were serving as auxiliaries to Roman legions and trading with settlements in Britain. Palladius preceded Patrick (c. 385–461) but through their joint efforts and those of Patrick's immediate followers, Ireland became the first country outside direct Roman influence to have a substantially Christian population. This happened in spite of established Celtic druids, pagan kings and petty chieftains with strong or motley armies and a fear of gods that demanded observance of certain rituals and customs. Dunmurry Hill, for example, formed part of an inner ring of fire that followed the Bealtaine fire of Uisneach in the centre of Ireland. This ring united all the provinces around Uisneach's 'Fire Eye' and signalled the lighting of the 'outer ring' on promontories around the coastline.

Being lawmakers, advisers to kings and educators of the young, druids held great influence. They also claimed healing powers and therefore supervised a form of religion before the introduction of Christianity. Slavery was common and Irish would have been the spoken language among the sparse population that occupied the area that now forms

Co. Kildare. An ascetic way of life provided a fruitful base upon which forceful personalities could build a rigorous Christianity.

BRIGID

Ireland's celebrated triumvirate of early saints contained two males, Patrick and Colmcille (c. 521–597). Completing it was one woman, Saint Brigid of Kildare (c. 453–523). Christianity adapted the ancient customs and pagan rituals to form a matrix for the proliferation of its own teaching. This allowed Patrick to introduce an episcopal system of church government, mainly in the north and west of Ireland. It followed the Roman method of establishing a petty kingdom as the basic unit. This was known as a tuath. The system adapted easily to the pockets of inhabitation that existed in Ireland, such as those in Co. Kildare.

After preaching in a region, Patrick selected a holy person who he then anointed as bishop to continue conversion. Eventually, this man acquired secular power. Patrick is alleged to have lived for some time on the site of the Church of Ireland in Naas. Visiting Old Kilcullen, tradition tells, he created a bishopric and put Bishop Mac Táil (d. 549) in charge. Patrick's companion, Saint Iserninus (d. 468), allegedly established a monastery there and the remains of crosses and a round tower mark its site. Another fifth century friend of Patrick's, Saint Auxilius, is credited with founding a house at Killashee (Cill Ausaile/Church of Auxilius), near Naas. Sinchell the Elder, who, like Mac Táil died in 549, had a monastery at Clane. Saint Ailbe of Ferns (d.c. 527) founded an abbey there. The 'wart stone' (a bullaun) at Clane may have been used for early baptisms. Christians believed that a stone from Lullymore monastery bore the footprint of Saint Patrick and that the saint established a church at Narraghmore.

Saint Colmcille's association with Co. Kildare was slight. He had connections with monasteries at Moone and Leixlip and his special embroiderer was the sixth century Saint Ercnaith or Coca, from which Kilcock (Cill Cóca/Coca's Church) receives its name. But the third saint of the triumvirate was enormously influential inside and outside the county.

Whitley Stokes (1830–1909) wrote:

Brigit was born at sunrise neither within nor without a house, was bathed in milk, her breath revives the dead, a house in which she is staying flames up to heaven, cow-dung blazes before her, oil is poured on her head; she is fed from the milk of a white, red-eared cow; a fiery pillar rises over her head; sun rays support her wet cloak; she remains a virgin and she was one of the two mothers of Christ the Anointed.[1]

Brigit, also Brigid, was a triune goddess of healing and smiths, but particularly of fertility. Emblematic of the Brigantes of Britain, the name means High or Exalted One. There was a connection between her feast day and the coming of milk into ewes, and indeed many customs connected with the Christian saint also had to do with animals' milk. There is a theory, therefore, that a Kildare convert to Christianity became a very holy woman, took the name of the fertility goddess and became the popularly-known Saint Brigid. Whatever her origin, Kildare's Saint Brigid is the most significant example of the progression from paganism to Christianity in Ireland. Her followers believed she had the power to intercede with the Christian God and in their hearts and minds she replaced her namesake goddess.

Because of her impact on Christianity in Kildare and elsewhere, some traditions concerning Brigid are worth exploring. They tell that her father, Dubhtach, was a descendant of Conn Céad Cathach (Con of the Hundred Battles) while her mother, Brochessian, was of the noble house of the O'Connors. Although a native of Faughart, Co. Louth, she established a great religious house in Kildare town after Saint Mel of Longford (d. 488) presented her with the veil of an abbess. Kildare people staunchly claim she was born at Umeras, near Kildare town.

The 'Mary of the Gael', 'Prophetess of Christ', 'Second Mother of Christ' or 'Queen of the South' is the inspiration for dozens of stories of miracles and wonders. The most common tells of her accepting a site by a high oak tree offered by Dunlang Mac Enda, King of Leinster. She built a church there and called the place Cill Dara, 'the church of the oak'. She required some extra land for her small community to farm. The King was not feeling too generous, so Brigid said, 'Just give me as much as my cloak will cover.' The King agreed and Brigid laid her cloak on the ground. It began spreading until it was covering the plain that is now the Curragh. The legend inspired a prayer to the saint:

A Bhrígid, scar os mo chionn	Brigid, spread above my head
Do bhrat fíonn dom anacal.	Your bright cloak for my protection.

A derivative is a common Irish saying: Fé bhrat Bhrígid go raibh tú (May you be [safe] under Brigid's cloak). The monastic community kept sheep on the Curragh and by weaving long white robes for themselves they may have introduced spinning.

SIMPLE FAITH

A tender story tells of Brigid's sadness while sitting one evening with a nun who had been blind since birth. She was heartbroken that her colleague could not see the magnificent sight before them. The rolling green plains were bathed in amber from a sinking sun and trees were shimmering in the glow. Brigid asked the Lord to grant her power to give her companion sight and then touched the nun's eyelids. The nun beheld the splendour of nature and praised God. Fearful that seeing such beautiful things might distract her from prayer, however, she asked Brigid to restore the blindness.

Animals gave Brigid great delight and she cured them regularly. She could tame wild boars and once she trained a fox to do tricks for her visitors' amusement. Brigid lit a fire within the convent grounds in Kildare which burned for six centuries, a perpetual flame of its time, symbolising the light of God. It never needed attention but twenty virgins kept vigil by it within a paled area into which no man was allowed entry. Giraldus Cambrensis recorded its existence in AD 1200. He also mentioned 'Brigid's Bird', a falcon that perched on the church tower and flew errands for the military and the townspeople. Monks wrote a book of the gospels in Kildare, Giraldus claimed, 'at the dictation of an angel during the lifetime of the virgin'. Aubrey De Vere (1788–1846) wrote:

> Saint Brigid is the mother, all men know,
> Of Erin's nuns that have been or shall be,
> From great Saint Patrick's time to that last day
> When Christ returns to judge the world with fire!
> Her life was full of miracles.

As the fame of Brigid's monastery spread, members of aristocratic households from home and abroad came to Kildare for the superior education that only monasteries were imparting at the time. There they could learn to read, write, fashion beautiful metal objects and adorn vellum and textiles with exquisite ornamentation. Each monastery developed a scriptorium where, in magnificent illuminated calligraphy, diaries of the community were kept, so initiating the writing of senchas (history). Kildare's would have been no exception.

Servicing this ever-expanding centre required labourers, traders and farmers, and so the population of the area grew. This in turn made it politically important and as a result the Kings of Leinster, then based at Naas, watched developments closely.

In her monastery Brigid hosted gatherings of the most important people in the land, religious and secular. She intervened in disputes and brought peace to warring factions. Clerics and chieftains, young and old, sought her advice on grave matters. Saint Kevin of Glendalough (498–618), Saint Brendan of Clonfert (483–577) and Saint Finian of Clonard (c. 454–552) visited her in Kildare. She cured the sick and continued giving alms generously. Brigid established convents all over Ireland and she and other nuns from Kildare went abroad. Her name crops up in chronicles from holy places in Scotland and on the continent.

The 'Saint Brigid's Cross', made of rushes, was a popular talisman in husbandry and in modern times became the symbol for the fledgling Irish broadcasting station, Radio Telefís Éireann. While it represents the Cross of Christ it also suggests the sun and its rays, a powerful pagan symbol. One story tells how the saint picked dead rushes off a cabin floor and wove it to bring about a deathbed conversion. Some villages in Co. Kildare observed the custom of appointing a virgin to represent the saint on her feast day. The young woman would bring the rush crosses and would speak a blessing in verse to each householder, who then placed the cross in the roof of a cow byre.

There was a custom of lighting 'Fires of Brigid' along the Red Hills between the Curragh and Rathangan on the first day of spring, 1 February, the Christian Saint Brigid's feast day. That day was also Imbolg, an important quarter-day in areas where the language was Goidelic (Irish, Scottish and Manx Gaelic.)

Another Saint Brigid founded a church at Oughterard, near Kill, in the sixth century.

CONLETH

There are suggestions that the Christian faith spread so rapidly in Co. Kildare after Brigid set up her convent that a paruchia (diocese) may have emerged as early as the year 490, and that bishops named Ivor and Lony ruled them. Most chroniclers agree, however, that Saint Conleth (Conlaed d. 519) was its first bishop. Of the Dál-Messincorb tribe, his was also known as Ronnchenn Mochanna-Daire. Conleth was living as a hermit in a cell at Old Connell, near the River Liffey at Newbridge, when Saint Patrick visited him and concluded that he would be an ideal co-ordinator for the propagation of the faith begun by Saint Brigid. Patrick informed Brigid, who befriended Conleth and enlisted his services. A great host of holy men and women attended his installation ceremony. Tradition suggests that, most atypically, Saint Brigid may have consecrated him as bishop. He willingly assisted Brigid, preaching and curing the sick. Monks and nuns lived separate lives within Brigid's monastery and Conleth led the male community there before becoming chaplain to all Brigid's convents and places of learning. These included a subject foundation on the southern edge of the Curragh at Kilbride (Cill Bríd/Brigid's Church).

Conleth made a pilgrimage to Rome and brought back precious vestments which he reserved for use only on feast days in honour of the Almighty or of the Apostles. Brigid found a more practical use for them: she gave them to the poor who would benefit by trading their expensive ornamentation. Conleth was skilled in crafting from gold and silver and is credited with fashioning the crosier of Saint Bérach of Termonbarry, a town on the Roscommon-Longford county border.

Tradition tells that a wolf attacked and killed Conleth on Lyons Hill, Celbridge, c. 519. His burial took place in the monastery grounds of Kildare and people who prayed to him or who visited his grave began claiming miracles. This led to his remains being exhumed and preserved in a bejewelled silver casket set into the high altar.

NINNIDH

Saint Ninnidh Lamghlann (of the unspotted hand) was a pupil of Conleth's and may have been born in Kildare town where he paid visits to Saint Brigid. Tradition tells how she told him she would receive the Holy Viaticum from him. Realising that this meant he would become a priest, Ninnidh thereafter kept his hand covered and received his nickname as a consequence. He received his education from Saint Fiach of Sleaty (Sletty, near Carlow town), in Britain and in Rome, where he may have received Holy Orders. Brigid's prophesy remained with him and he stayed away from Kildare as long as possible so that she would live to a great age. He did return, the story goes, in time to administer the last rites.

DIOCESES AND HOLY MEN

If Conleth's installation took place in the fifth century, as seems likely, Kildare may have been the earliest Leinster diocese. However, a Pontifical Yearbook (*Anno Pontificio*) entry places its establishment in the sixth, in the year of Saint Conleth's death. Highly regarded, its administration included an archdeacon, dean, treasurer, chanter and chancellor. The title Archbishop of the Province of Leinster first belonged to Sleaty (see above), then to Ferns in Co. Wexford. It transferred to the Prelate of Kildare in the seventh century. Although not all its bishops' names have been recorded, the dioceses has had unbroken succession since Conleth, currently as the diocese of Kildare and Leighlin (Roman Catholic) and Meath and Kildare (Church of Ireland. See Religion, Chapter 7).

Other people of sanctity participated in the Christianisation of Co. Kildare. Bishop Auxilius of Killashee (see above) probably chose his site to benefit from the protection of the Leinster king who resided nearby in Naas. Saint Ercnaith or Coca of Kilcock (see Brigid, above) was sixth century as was Saint Eimhín of Munster who gave his name to Monasterevin (Mainistir Eimhín. See Chapter 9). The monastery he founded there became Ros Glas or Ros Glaise an Muimhnach (The Munster man's Green Wood. See Men of the Land of Loughs, Chapter 4). Eimhín is often credited with authorship of *The Tripartite Life of Saint Patrick*. Maeldubh, who fostered Saint Fechin of Fore (d.c. 665), Co. Westmeath, was also associated with Monasterevin. Later he became Abbot of Durrow in Offaly and later still occupied a cell near the Royal Saxon palace of Ingleburne, Wiltshire, England, where he was called Maeldulph. When he died and was buried there it became Maeldulph's Bury, later Malmesbury.

An ancient 'Litany of Angus the Culdee' included Seven Holy Bishops of Drom Airchaille, a name associated with Co. Kildare's smallest parish of Dunmurraghill, Donadea, that occupied just over 165 hectares. A stone (*Petra Patricii*) there pronounced a visit from the patron and a Martar-Teach (Relic House) gave its name to a place called 'The Reliceen'.

Dendrochronological studies from the Bog of Allen and elsewhere have led modern scientists to believe that widespread restricted growth occurred again in the mid-fifth century. They have concluded that there was extreme lack of sunlight and that famine and plague ravaged Western Europe, including Ireland. Volcanic dust may have been the cause of this because slivers of tephra, or volcanic glass, have been found in peat formed during that period between Rathangan and Edenderry. A comet strike has also been suggested. The cult of the relic may have entered the Christian psyche during this period of travail.

FURTHER DEVELOPMENTS

By the end of the fifth century there were many Christianised communities in Ireland and Irish missionaries were beginning to go abroad to spread the gospel. During the centuries that followed, the longing for spiritual solace and hope that accompanies disasters assisted the propagation of Christianity at home and abroad. Before continuing a chronological examination of Kildare's history, it might be useful to note here some developments in Christianity during the centuries following its establishment.

Monks were commonly associated with fasting and praying between hours of painstaking calligraphic preparation of illuminated manuscripts and fashioning sacred objects. They performed these skills in small wattle cells clustered around their abbot's larger cell. Being self-sufficient, they also manufactured tools to till the earth and reap its produce. Some were stone carvers and a ninth century High Cross excavated at Moone in 1835 and pieced together bears witness to the continuing eminence of a sixth century Columban monastery there. High Crosses bore carvings to illustrate aspects of religion to an illiterate people. Those on the Moone High Cross depict Saint Anthony, Saint Paul, the Twelve Apostles, the Crucifixion, the Three Hebrews in the Furnace, the Flight into Egypt and the miracle of the Loaves and Fishes—with a pair of eels as side servings!

During the sixth and seventh centuries, monastic and anchoritic foundations flourished. Dispersed communities, recognising the most influential abbot in the vicinity, formed alliances that dictated episcopal succession. Units retained the name fairche, Irish for parish. Throughout this period the functions of successors to Saint Patrick's bishops were becoming more sacramental.

Cogitosus, a seventh century Kildare monk, described Kildare town as 'a vast metropolitan city'. In that century celebrated personages like Abbot Lochéne Sapiens (d. 696) were visiting Kildare. Saint Moling (d.c. 697), often credited with having Leinster subjects exempted from the dreaded Bóramha tribute, established a monastery in Timolin (Tí Mólin/Moling's House) which Arroasian nuns later occupied from 1200 to 1541 (see Church and State, Chapter 4). A Kildare man, Folachtach from Teach Túa (Taghado/Túa's house, near Maynooth) was abbot of Clonmacnoise when he died in 765. Castledermot (Díseart Díarmaid/ Dermot's hermitage) was the site of an eighth/ninth century foundation by Saint Díarmaid (d. 823). Like the Moone High Cross, two High Crosses at Castledermot include carvings of Saints Paul and Anthony, the Twelve Apostles and the Crucifixion. The Sacrifice of Isaac and Daniel in the Lions Den are among other themes. Saint Laurence O'Toole (c. 1130–1180) (see Church and State, Chapter 4), a Castledermot man, received the sacrament of baptism there in 1130.

There have been claims that the poet and Greek and Latin scholar Sedulius Scotus (fl. 840–855) visited Kildare monastery. The Irish form of Sedulius is, however, Siadhal and there was an abbot of that name (d. 828) in Kildare. Twenty-five bishops ruled Kildare before the Synod of Kells in 1152 instituted a formation of dioceses which has changed little since then (see Religion, Chapter 7).

Clane Abbey was built on the site of a monastery that, in 1162, hosted a general Church synod. Gelasius, who was Archbishop of Armagh from 1137 to 1174, was among twenty-six bishops and a large number of abbots who attended. Paranoid about being poisoned, he brought his own white cow along and drank nothing but its milk and refused the food offered by his hosts. The first Archbishop of Dublin, Laurence O'Toole, had just been appointed and was present. The synod decreed that only men educated in Armagh could be appointed lectors throughout Ireland and that only Armagh-trained Masters of Studies should be appointed to monasteries. This bestowed on Armagh a prestige that lasted for centuries. Seven years later, Rory O'Connor, the last authentic High King of Ireland (d. 1198), exacted stipends to make the decree viable.

There was an early monastery at Kilteel, near Rathcoole. Some historians claim that Saint Ninian (also associated with Monasterevin) founded a monastery in Cloncurry, near Kilcock, early in the fifth century, but a medieval Carmelite foundation is more firmly recognised. Cornelius Mac Gelain (d. 1223), a Bishop of Kildare, was buried there.

The Franciscan order founded a friary in Castledermot sometime before 1247. Thomas, Lord of Ossory, financially assisted its development in 1302. Edward Bruce plundered it in 1317 and it was suppressed in 1540. The friars returned in 1639 and were expelled by Cromwell's army in 1639. Returning in 1661, they remained until the mid-eighteenth century. Another Franciscan friary, the Grey Abbey in Kildare town, had a similar history. It became the traditional burial place of the Earls of Kildare (see Geraldines, Chapter 4). Suppressed in 1539, the O'Connors destroyed some of its buildings in 1540. The friars returned in 1621 and, apart from abandonment during the Cromwellian campaign, the institution survived for over 150 years.

The Irish missionary tradition had developed and education given at Kildare was playing a major role in spreading the culture of learning in Europe. 'Pilgrims of Christ' were setting up communities in Bobbio (Italy), Luxeuil (France) and Pérona Scottorum (Péronne of the Irish, France).

RELIGIOUS ART

A fusion of Irish-Latin influences in religious art and ornamentation was significant. Artists who had previously fashioned beautifully embellished weapons and implements for nobles, began making ornate chalices and other items for worship. Stonemasons were using their skills to carve representations of religious episodes. Jacques-Paul Migne (1800–1875) wrote about the tombs of Brigid and Conleth on either side of the altar in Kildare Abbey that were richly ornamented with gold, silver and precious gems. They have also pictorial representations in relief and in colours, and are surmounted by crowns of gold and silver,' [2] he wrote.

Christianity continued to flourish in Co. Kildare (see Development of Christianity, Chapter 4) where the main centres of Irish religious education would emerge.

HOLY WELLS

Unkind critics of a gaudily dressed woman would often say 'she's like a bush at a holy well'. This was because people who claimed cures often left strips of clothing to vouch for their miracle. Seeking supernatural assistance in illness by drinking waters is a tradition that dates back to the arrival of Christianity and, in some cases, to the pre-Christian period. There are over seventy such wells in Co. Kildare. Up to the mid-nineteenth century a pattern was held at Saint Colman's well on the slopes of the Hill of Allen. Saint Brigid's well at Tully, near Kildare town, still attracts pilgrims. Trinity Well at Carbury, the source of the River Boyne, is a holy well and a pilgrimage or pattern held there on Trinity Sunday was once a major gathering. A pattern and faction fighting were features of annual pilgrimages to Saint Patrick's Well at Glassealy, near Ballitore. Father Moore's Well on the Curragh's edge at Rathbride is more modern. Allegedly, Father Moore performed miracles and when he died in 1826, visits to a well near his cottage began. The momentary wearing of his hat became an accepted cure for headaches.

NORSE,
4 NORMAN *and*
GERALDINE

CO. KILDARE'S HISTORY can never be treated in isolation. The county played a significant role in major national dramas. Originally, Ireland had five cúige (provinces): Laighin, Mumhain, Connachta, Midhe and Uladh (Leinster, Munster, Connaught, Meath and Ulster). The eastern province, once called Galian, may have taken the name Laighin from Liath, son of a Nemenian called Laigne Lethan Glas. It may also have Gallic origins, because Gauls called their distinctive blue-green spear a laighen. Norse settlers added 'stadr' (a place), so Laighin-ster became Anglicised to Leinster. Tír, however, means 'country' so a Gaelic influence on the evolution of the name cannot be ruled out.

From the middle of the fifth to the middle of the eleventh centuries Leinster corresponded roughly to parts of the present counties Kildare, Carlow and Wicklow and most of Wexford. The Carbury area of Co. Kildare, however, was in the kingdom of Meath

Co. Kildare's early septs included the O'Toole (of Hy Muireadhaigh), O'Byrne (of Uí Fáeláin), O'Keary (or O'Carey, of Uí Cairpri Laigin) and, MacKeogh.

The *Annals of Lough Cé* relate that Leinster's kings came mainly from tribes that congregated around the Curragh. They ruled from strongholds there and at Naas and Kilcullen. Battles with the men of Breagh (part of

Meath), particularly across the Rye river at Leixlip, were common. Some areas, notably Wexford, were almost independent, however, and on occasions when Wexford's Hy Kinsella (Uí Chennselaigh) were kings of Leinster they suffered the resentment of Kildare and most of north Leinster and came under attack from neighbouring Ossory. This rivalry was to have a significant effect on subsequent events.

A great fire burned Kildare town c. 709. In 722, High King Fergal of Tara (d. 722) led an invasion force of over 20,000 Meath men into Leinster. Murchad Mac Bran (d. 727), Leinster's king, sited his 9,000 strong army in a defensive position around the Hill of Allen which was the only suitable terrain for defence, and if Fergal penetrated their lines he would force the Leinster men out of Kildare. Mac Bran's men fought valiantly and there were heavy losses on both sides, but when Fergal fell in the battle the Meath men retreated.

MEN OF The LAND OF LOUGHS

In 795 the first Norsemen came. They were also called Vikings, Lochlannaigh (Men of the Land of Loughs) or, inaccurately, 'Danes', because Ireland's invaders were mainly from Norway. They landed at 'Reachrainn', which may have been Rathlin Island, north of Antrim, or Lambay Island, east of Dublin, but they certainly reached Innishmurray off Sligo and destroyed it in 807. Leinster was fertile ground for their activities because the Laighin (Leinstermen) had never accepted lordship from the feuding Uí Néill at Tara or from the Eóganachta at Cashel. The death in Kildare of Fínsneachta Catharderc (d. 808), who had regained the High Kingship of Leinster in 806 brought more internal dynastic strife to Leinster. The *Annals of the Four Masters* described the Norsemen as 'merciless, soure and hardie, from their very cradles dissentious'. The Irish were already aware of this because missionaries in Lindisfarne and on the Northumbrian coast of England had suffered their onslaughts two years previously.

Ireland's dark visitors ravaged, plundered and killed the Irish or took them away to sell into slavery. They settled around coastal cities and large river estuaries, but their long boats were able to navigate shallow waters as well as rough seas. Although in 824 the monastic community at Kildare was able to attack Tallaght, near Dublin, according to the

Annals of the Four Masters the Norsemen's craft were on the River Boyne and on the River Liffey. They ravaged 'every church and abbey within the territories of Magh Liffe and Magh Breagh.' Clane beat them off but '[in 836] they raided [Kildare town] with fire and sword and carried off the shrines of Saint Brigid and Saint Conleth.'[1] Historians question a claim that Brigid's remains were safely interred in Downpatrick, Co. Down, at this stage. Also in 836, Feidlimid mac Crimhthainn (d. 847), the king-bishop of Cashel who was challenging the rulers at Tara and, like the Norsemen, was destroying monasteries, raided Kildare. He had a meeting with the High King at Cloncurry in 838.

The invaders began forming a settlement in Dublin in 841 which gradually became their main centre of trade and a base for attacking neighbouring areas. In 844 they struck at Kildare town, murdering its Prior, Kethern. Their warrior, Turges, or Turgesius (d. 845) had ideas of becoming King of Ireland and stories concerning his rampages abound. There is evidence, however, that he had sixty long boats on the River Boyne and the River Liffey.

Some commentators believe that the tyrant was a mythical figure conceived to exaggerate the valour of King Malachy (d. 862) and other Irish leaders who confronted him. Malachy (Máel Sechnaill I) was High King of Ireland from 846 (formally recognised in 859) to 862. Malachy's drowning of Turgesius in Lough Owel, Co. Westmeath is, however, a recognised fact.

ROUND TOWERS

Round towers may have emerged at about this time as defences for monastic communities, although some historians dispute this. One view suggests that their high doors were designed for the defence of a community by pulling up a ladder after entry. Another view is that the high bases were required for structural stability. Their use as bell towers and as repositories for books and documents is recognised, but whatever their true functions, round towers at Castledermot, Taghadoe and Kildare are still in evidence. During the 1998–99 laying of the Clane gas pipe medieval window segments and local ware came to light. These artifacts serve as a reminder of the importance of Kildare in medieval times.

MORE STRIFE

In 861 Dublin Norsemen killed Muiregan, son of the Lord of Naas. Irish rule was then vested in two powerful dynasties. Because the northern Uí Néill ruled from Tara and the southern Eóghanachta from Cashel, control of Leinster became the most critical requirement for anyone aspiring to outright rule of Ireland. One bishop-king of Munster, Cormac Mac Cuilenáin (836–908) crossed the border of Uí Néill territory at Monasterevin in 908 and claimed jurisdiction over Ros Glas monastery (see Chapter 3). This caused the Battle of Ballaghmoon, on the Carlow border, where kings of Tara, Leinster and Connaught combined to rout the allied armies of Munster and Ossory. Cormac lost both the battle and his life. Some claim that he was buried in Castledermot (later, at the dawn of the twelfth century, the King of Uí Fáilghe, Dermot O'Dempsey, introduced the Cistercian order at Ros Glas, the first of many continental religious orders to arrive).

The Dublin Norsemen continued to invade, plundering most of Co. Kildare in 916, occupying towns and giving them the configuration of those they had seen in northern Europe. The High King of the time was Niall Glúndubh. When the self-styled High King Domhnall (Uí Néill) died in 980, the Uí Néill nominated Malachy the Great (Máel Sechnaill II, d. 1022) of Meath as king. But he was facing the challenge of an ambitious Munster man, Brian Ború (c. 941–1014) who was already subduing small uprisings in Leinster and preventing the further spread of Norse influence. Leinster became their arena and the men of Ossory supported Brian Ború.

Olaf 'The Sandal' (Cuarán, d.c. 980) ruled Dublin for forty years. As an old man he married Gormflaith (d. 1030), the daughter of Murchadha, Lord of Naas (Nás). The union bore Sitric (d. 1042) who was to play a significant role in the life of Brian Ború. Before his death, Olaf recruited reserve troops from Scotland and the Isle of Man for an attack on Meath. Malachy II defeated him at Tara in 980 and Olaf journeyed to Iona on pilgrimage and died there. Malachy occupied Dublin but allowed Sitric to remain as its ruler in return for paying considerable tribute. In a strategic move, Malachy married Gormflaith. Murchadha had been killed and his son Maol Mórdha (d. 1014 at the Battle of Clontarf, see below) was Lord of Naas. With his sister Gormflaith as virtual queen of Dublin he may have had his sights on the kingship of Leinster.

In the final years of the tenth century, Sitric attacked Kildare town and ravaged it. Almost simultaneously, Maol Mórdha became King of Leinster. Some commentators argue that Brian Ború nominated him while others point out that if Brian had the power to nominate, he would have won a valuable ally by installing an enemy rather than an adherent. In any event, Maol Mórdha made the contemptible decision to offer Leinster's fealty and resources to Sitric. This shock convinced the warring Brian Ború and Malachy that they should unite. In 999 their combined forces took on the Leinster army at Gleann Máma (Glenn of the Pass). Some suggest that this was in Wicklow, but a more likely site was in the Kill-Rathcoole area, between Kildare's Newcastle-Lyons-Oughterard ridges and those of Saggart. This ideal battleground is still used in military exercises for students in the Curragh's Military College.

Malachy and Brian routed the enemy. Brian's son Murchadha discovered the Lord of Naas hiding in a tree but spared him, foolishly as it transpired. Brian had a close relationship with Gormflaith. Under the liberal Brehon Laws he may even have married her, because she was estranged from Malachy at the time. Expediently, he gave his daughter's hand to Sitric who submitted to him.

At the Battle of Clontarf on Good Friday, 23 April 1014, old rivalry resurfaced when north Leinster forces sided with the Norsemen against Brian Ború. Although victorious, Brian was killed after it. Returning from the encounter, the armies of Desmond and Thomond camped at Magh Maistean, a plain near Athy. The traditional dispute about the kingship of Munster, then held by Thomond, erupted. The Desmondites realised that Thomond casualties at Clontarf were considerable and that their king of Munster was wounded, so they demanded that a Desmond king be appointed to rule Munster. While both sides were preparing for action, Thomond's wounded were brought to Mullamast for safety. They resented being left out of battle, however, and allegedly stuffed their wounds with moss before returning to join in the action. Their bravery scared the men of Desmond into withdrawing from hostilities and continuing their march southward. The men of Thomond brought their gallant comrades to Athy and washed their wounds in the waters of the River Barrow.

TERRITORIAL CLAIMS

The smallest territorial division at that time was the seisreach or ploughland of about 49.5 hectares. Next came the baile—either a house or its steward's sub-division (ballybetagh) of about two and twelve ploughlands, respectively. The tuath was a district of about 360 ploughlands belonging to a sept (a family and its retainers) led by a chief who could field 700 men. A mór tuath was about four times that size and was the equivalent to an English Riding. The Brehon Laws laid down strict rules for appointing Chiefs and their deputy Tánaistí.

The ancient Gaelic septs of Co. Kildare were descended from Cathaeir Mór, King of Ireland (d.c. 122). The Uí Fáilghe (O'Connors Faly) ruled over the present baronies of East and West Offaly and part of Co. Laois. Their inaugurations probably took place on the hill formation known as the Chair of Kildare on the east of Dunmurry Hill. They lost some of their lands to the FitzGeralds (see The Geraldines, below) during the Anglo-Norman invasion, and the remainder during the plantations of Co. Laois and Co. Offaly. O'Connor comes from Conchobhar, meaning 'wolf-lover', and was a common early Irish name.

From the Uí Fáilghe line evolved two prominent branches, the O'Dempseys, (from the Irish word diomasach, meaning proud) and the O'Dunnes, (from the Irish word donn, meaning brown-haired.) Dunne is still a common name throughout Co. Kildare. The powerful O'Byrne sept was also driven from Co. Kildare into south Co. Wicklow as a result of the Anglo-Norman invasion.

CHURCH AND STATE

Throughout medieval times in Kildare town the vigilant nuns kept Saint Brigid's perpetual fire alight. The town was still growing, one of a number of small inland centres engaged in local commerce and providing depots in a network for delivering and receiving goods from Dublin harbour. The Synod of Ráth Breasail in Munster (1111) recognised Kildare as a new diocese with its own cathedral. Within a decade the cathedral was in ruins and remained so until Bishop Ralph of Bristol (d. 1232), who was Bishop of Kildare from 1223 to 1232, built a new one. It survived until the seventeenth century.

At the Synod of Kells (1152), Ireland was divided into its present pattern of dioceses. Some twenty-five bishops had then ruled Kildare since Saint Conleth's time. The Synod confirmed Finn O'Gorman (d. 1177) as Bishop of Kildare. This scholarly man had compiled *The Book of Leinster*, an anthology of poetry and fable, between 1130 and 1150 and had been acting bishop of Kildare since 1148.

In Mullachreelan Woods, three miles north of Castledermot, Laurence O'Toole was born. He grew up to become abbot of the Celtic monastery at Glendalough (1153) and archbishop of Dublin (1162). He died in Au in France and was canonised in 1225.

Dermot MacMurrough (1110–1171) was King of Leinster in 1132 when he sacked Kildare town and its abbey, maltreating its abbess disgracefully. The abbey recovered and in the latter part of that century Giraldus Cambrensis (c. 1147–1223) wrote of a miraculous book he saw there 'which they say was written at the dictation of an angel.' The book contained the concordance of the four gospels that Saint Jerome translated from Hebrew when domiciled in Bethlehem. It may have contained early expressionist illustration because the Welsh traveller described:

> Here you can look upon the face of the divine majesty drawn in a miraculous way. Here too upon the mystical representations of the Evangelists, now having six, now four, and now two, wings. Here you will see the eagle; there a calf. Here the face of a man; there that of a lion. And there are almost innumerable other drawings. If you look at them carelessly and casually and not too closely, you may judge them to be mere daubs rather than careful compositions. You will see nothing subtle where everything is subtle. But if you take the trouble to look very closely, and penetrate with your eyes the secrets of the artistry, you will notice such intricacies, so delicate and subtle, so close together and well knitted, so involved and bound together, and so fresh still in their colourings that you will not hesitate to declare that all these things must have been the work, not of men but of angels.[2]

Cambrensis went on to describe Kildare town with its round tower and marvellous manuscript as well as legends of Saint Brigid. He also mentioned 'soldiers of the castle' and the earliest recording of what probably would have been an earthwork castle.

T*he* NORMANS

The original Normans were from Normandy in Northern France. They conquered England in 1066. Those who invaded Ireland were mainly Welsh settlers or Cambro-Normans. As mercenaries, they accompanied the deposed and exiled King of Leinster, Dermot MacMurrough, in his 1167 repatriation. MacMurrough had ruled Leinster since the death of his father Énna in 1126. There were two possible causes for his exile. MacMurrough abducted Dervorgilla (d. 1172), wife of Tigernán Ua Ruairc, who was Lord of Breifne (1124–1172). Ua Ruairc may have deposed him in a bid to extend his area of power. A more likely reason was MacMurrough's ambition to become High King of Ireland. Rory O'Connor, the incumbent since 1166, beat off his attempt and added Leinster to his Connaught kingship.

After being deposed, MacMurrough went abroad to enlist aid from King Henry II (1133–1189). He received permission to raise an army in Wales. In 1169 Maurice FitzGerald (d. 1177) brought 100 infantrymen and archers, thirty men-at-arms and ten knights to Ireland, landing at Bannow, Co. Wexford (his half-brother, Robert FitzStephen (d.c. 1182) had arrived a few months earlier). FitzGerald was the second son of Gerald FitzWalter (d.c. 1135), Constable of Pembroke Castle and brother of David (1147–1176), bishop of Saint David's, Wales. As a reward, he received the eastern portion of the O'Byrne territory of Offelan, making him Baron of Naas and Lord of Maynooth.

MacMurrough's main ally, however, was Strongbow (Richard FitzGilbert, also Richard de Clare, c. 1130–1176), a man who had been disgruntled since King Henry II deprived him of the Earldom of Pembroke in 1154. In 1170, Strongbow landed at Passage, Co. Waterford and moved quickly to occupy Waterford city. He swept up to Dublin and reinstated MacMurrough who offered his daughter's hand in marriage. Strongbow accepted and married this woman, Aoife (c. 1152–1189) in 1170. When MacMurrough died the following year, Strongbow became Lord of Leinster. This instigated the serious involvement of England in Irish affairs, because of fears that the Norman settlers might set up a rival dynasty in Ireland. Strongbow made Kildare the centre of his campaign to conquer Leinster.[3]

A concerned Henry II sent an expeditionary force to Ireland. After some parleying, the king agreed to Strongbow's retention of lordship of Leinster and of Strigoil (Chepstow in Monmouthshire, his Welsh keep).

Henry still refused to restore the Earldom of Pembroke to him, however. Through force of arms then, Strongbow settled Welsh and English allies in Leinster, including Co. Kildare. Aoife bore him a son, Gilbert (d.c. 1185) and a daughter, Isabella (1172–1220) who, in 1189, married William Marshal I (1147–1219). Marshal thereby acquired the lordship of Leinster, Chepstow and Strigoil. Ten years later, Marshal also recovered the Earldom of Pembroke that Strongbow had lost. His son, William II (1190–1231) had no heir, so succession went to his brothers Richard (d. 1234), Gilbert (d. 1241) and Walter (d. 1245). The Leinster lordship was eventually divided into administrative shires between the daughters of William Marshal I. Kildare went to Sybil (Sibilla), but by the time the division materialised in 1247 she was dead and Kildare was shared between her seven daughters. One of them, Agnes (d. 1290), married Baron William de Vescy. In 1278 Agnes had the liberty of Kildare (which also administered the present counties of Offaly and Laois) restored. When she died, her son William (d. 1297) inherited it. He became Lord Justice of Ireland (1290 to 1294). De Vescy surrendered the liberty of Kildare to the Crown in 1297 and Kildare became a Royal shire.

Meanwhile a parliament sat in Castledermot in 1264 and in Kildare town in 1276 and the Leinster Irish burned Narragh and Ardscull in 1286 and Rathangan in 1297.

The new landowners recognised the need for defence and constructed fortified homes or castles at Blackhall, Oughterard, Kilteel, Firmount, Blackwood and elsewhere. They built churches and restored old Celtic edifices at Kill, Killashee and Clane, to name a few. Where there were no suitable premises in which to pray, they erected them. Their architecture reflected that seen in Welsh places of worship, and the ruins at Kerdiffstown, Sherlockstown and Bodenstown bear witness.

Strongbow granted Naas and Offelan to Maurice FitzGerald. Maurice's grand daughter married David de Laundres, of a powerful Glamorganshire family, who also became Lord of Naas. The names De Burgh, Brewes, de Veele, Allan, Maunsel, Pierce and Osbert testify to the Cambro-Norman influence in Co. Kildare.

REWARDS, PUNISHMENTS AND MORE MONASTERIES

Offering the Lordship of Ireland became beneficial to kings wishing to repay favours or to displace men who posed a threat. English kings accommodated men like Hugh de Lacy (d. 1186) in 1172; William de Burg (d. 1205) in 1185 and William de Braose (d. 1211) in 1201. They in turn accommodated religious orders. Under a charter granted by the Diarmait Ua Dunmusaigh, King of Uí Fáilghe, Cistercians came to Monasterevin (c. 1178) and Augustinians and Arroasian nuns arrived in Graney and Timolin, respectively (c. 1200). These nuns also had houses at Rathkeale, Co. Limerick and at Kildoo and the Skelligs in Co. Kerry. They would have come from Missenden Abbey at Great Missenden, Buckinghamshire.

Myler FitzHenry (d. 1220) established a cell of the Welsh Llanthony Prima at Great Connell near Newbridge (c. 1202). As the Augustinian Priory of Our Lady and Saint David it was to become one of Ireland's most important monastic settlements. Its abbots represented religious orders in Parliament, the prior being a Lord Spiritual of Parliament. Great Connell cemetery contained a mitred effigy of Walter Wellesley, a prior who was also Bishop of Kildare (1529–40).

Richard de St Michael (d. 1242), Lord of Rheban, lived at Woodstock Castle. He founded Athy's Saint John's Priory of Augustinian Cruciferi c. 1216 and possibly the town's earlier Dominican friary. Later in the century, through marriage, the family's manor house at Athy and the Woodstock estate close by passed to the mighty House of Kildare (see The Geraldines, below).

Franciscans arrived in Kilcullen and Gerald FitzMaurice FitzGerald founded the order's Grey Abbey in Kildare town, c. 1254–60. The abbey housed the *Liber Albus*. That work included the writings of Aristotle, a history of the Franciscans and medieval manuscripts and lists. By 1328 the Grey Abbey had a Lady Chapel to assist obsequies and its church-yard became the burial place of up to ten Earls of Kildare. Joan deBurgo assisted a significant enlargement c. 1350 (see Further Developments, Chapter 3). FitzGerald also founded a Franciscan house in Clane (c. 1258) where his effigy later lay. Carmelites and Dominicans also came to Co. Kildare, establishing themselves in Kildare town and Athy.

In Naas, a new parish church dedicated to the Patron of Wales, Saint David, replaced Saint Patrick's, symbolising the Cambro-Norman influence on Christianity. Indeed, up to the beginning of the nineteenth century, Naas people wore a leek on Saint David's Day (1 March) in honour of the Welsh saint. (The tradition continued to the extent that in the nineteenth century a Welsh Regiment was marching through the town on 1 March and, thinking the locals were ridiculing them, began a fracas. On hearing the explanation, they embraced the Naas people.)

Henry III (1207–1272; King 1216–72), received large revenues from extensive Irish settlements. His successor was Edward I (1239–1307; King 1272–1307). Edward prudently appointed de Vescy Justiciar (see Glossary) as well as Lord of Offelan, so displacing John FitzThomas FitzGerald (see The Normans, above, and The Geraldines, below). John was already attempting to annex parts of Connaught and was furious at this new danger from his eastern flank which he resisted vigorously. Armed conflict seemed inevitable when Edward enlisted the aid of John de Wogan (d. 1321), lord of Picton Castle, Pembrokeshire. Wogan came to Ireland and calmed the situation by redefining areas of control. Cleverly, he and Edward persuaded de Vescy to yield Kildare but repossess it for his own lifetime. For his pains, Wogan became Justiciar from 1295 to 1308. He was campaigning vigorously in Co. Kildare (1305). During that period 'The Treacherous Baron', Piers de Bermingham, murdered Muirchartach O'Conchubhair Fáilge (O'Connor Faly) and his brother, In Calbach, together with eleven of their leaders at a banquet in Carrickoris Castle, Carbury.

The Wogan family would remain important in the north of the county until the mid-nineteenth century, and as Wogan Brownes when they married into the Browne family (see Clongowes Wood College, Chapter 7). Edward granted patents for markets, including one in 1286 on the green outside the Gerald FitzMaurice FitzGerald castle in Maynooth that was to become the seat of the FitzGeralds, Earls of Kildare, and where hangings took place. More correctly, Maynooth's square Norman castle could be termed a donjon after the style that originated in the Loire region of France. (Corruption of that designation and connotation produced the word 'dungeon' for the English language.) The ruins of Maynooth Castle are a permanent reminder of the Anglo-Norman FitzGerald dynasty (see The Geraldines, below) that had such an influence on events in Ireland, Leinster and Kildare.

A COUNTY EMERGING

Ireland's local government structure followed the English pattern with the county sheriff acting as local agent of the Crown. But while English shires had hundreds of sub-divisions, Ireland's equivalent counties contained larger cantreds, like the Welsh *cantref*. In many cases these later became baronies. Their evolution was haphazard. Only three sheriffs existed by 1212. They were in charge of Dublin (ruling Kildare), Waterford/Cork and the remainder of Munster (ruling from Limerick). There were no clearly outlined territories. King Henry II allowed Strongbow to create liberties and Kildare became one.

Regional formation was in a state of flux, gravitating towards development around towns and taking on the configuration of the tuath. More sheriffs began officiating in Kerry, Louth, Roscommon and the rest of Connaught. The sheriff's tasks included administration of justice and revenue collection. He had a coroner who, as well as holding inquests, kept a record of court cases that required a hearing from a visiting eyre of justicar. The sheriff's immediate subordinate, the chief-serjeant, supervised the activities of each cantred serjeant within the shire.

Although counties Meath and Kildare were formally constituted in 1297, their boundaries had begun emerging c. 1196. Seathrún Céitinn (Geoffrey Keating c. 1570–1649) described the northern boundary with Meath as running 'from Dublin to the Abhainn Righe [the River Rye that enters the Liffey at Leixlip after flowing through Kilcock, Maynooth and Carton] westward to Cluain Conrach (Cloncurry) [and on to] the Ford of the French Mill ... to Clonard ... to the Tocher of Carbury ... to Crannach Geishille (Geashill)'.[4]

In 1210 King John (1167–1216) defined seven Leinster counties from existing tuatha. In Co. Kildare these tuatha were Cairbre Ui Ciardha (Carbury), a small area in the north-west; Ui Faeláin (Offelan) bordering Meath, Dublin and part of Wicklow (this large portion was later divided into almost seven baronies. See below); Hy Muireadhaigh (Ormurethi) in the southern panhandle; and about half of Ui Fáilghe (Offaly) in the west. As noted, before 1296, Kildare had been under the jurisdiction of the Sheriff of Dublin, but as a result of the re-drawing of Dublin and Meath sheriffdoms in 1297, the lordship of Kildare became a shire or county. In Naas in 1345 the liberty of Kildare was formally returned to the Crown (see The Normans, above) and the following year Walter de Bermingham became Justiciar.

BARONIES

Early baronies were closely related to cantreds or smaller divisions represented by Gaelic tuatha and townlands. The historian Walter FitzGerald was a regular contributor to the *Journal of County Kildare Archaeological Society*. In Vol. III. No. 5, he listed the baronies as they existed in 1350:

Barony de Norragh
Barony de Ryban } now the two baronies of Narragh and Rheban
Barony de Donlost

Barony de Okathy } now the Barony of Ikeathy and Oughterany.
Barony de Oughtryn

Barony de Offaly, now the two baronies of East and West Offaly.

Barony de Kilca } now the Barony of Kilkea and Moone.
Barony de Mone

Barony de Conall, now Connell.

Barony de Carbery, now Carbury.

Barony de Otymy, now the Barony of Clane.

Barony de Kilcolyn, now Kilcullen.

Barony de Maynotheslee } now the two baronies of North and South Salt.
Barony del Sant

Barony del Naas } now the two baronies of North and South Naas.
Barony de Rathmore

He went on to say:

> *I have not been able to identify the ancient barony of 'Donlost'; this place-name is now obsolete. I have met . . . the name [in] Archbishop Alen's 'Crede Mihi' (a Register in which are copied documents mainly dealing with the thirteenth and*

fourteenth centuries). In the list of churches included in the then Deanery of Athy appear, among others, the 'Ecclesia de Donbren, Capella de Dunloste'; so that the barony of Donlost may have been that portion of the barony of Narragh and Rheban West which lies on the Queen's Co. side of the Barrow, and adjoining which are the townlands of Dunbrin Upper and Lower.

As to the barony of 'Otymy', this name is also obsolete, but it corresponds with the present barony of Clane. A Co. Kildare Chancery Inquisition makes mention of 'the Manor of Clane, alias Otmany,' in 1617. In 'Otymy' was situated a district called 'Arst', in which lay 'Donnyng,' i.e., Downings; and in 1399 James de Ponkeston was given the custody of the Manor of Ballykeppagh, the lands of Cloughgan, Stableriston, Blackhall in Arst and a watermill in Clane. . . . In the thirteenth century 'Otymy' was a lordship belonging to Adam de Hereford.

The old barony called 'Maynotheslee' was in the FitzGerald territory. After the rebellion of the Silken Thomas, John and Thomas Alen (of Saint Wolstan's and Kilteel) were appointed for life Constables and Keepers of the King's Castle of Maynoth, seneschals of the Court, surveyors and keepers of the Manor of Maynoth and Maynothesley and of the woods and forests there, as well as Rangers and Keepers of the Park of Maynoth. The name Maynotheslee means the leas or fields of Maynooth; the latter portion of the name is to be found in Broad'leas and White'leas, formerly portions of the Ballymore Eustace commons.

The Barony 'del Sant' is now called Salt, a contraction of the Latin Saltus Sahnonum, alias Leixlip, or the Salmon Leap.[5]

The baronies therefore became Carbury, Clane, Connell, East Offaly, Ikeathy and Oughterany, Kilcullen, Kilkea and Moone, Narragh and Rheban East, Narragh and Rheban West, North Naas, South Naas, North Salt, South Salt, West Offaly.

The transition, however, was not smooth. In 1300, for example, the Irish burned Athy and Edward Bruce (d. 1318, see The Geraldines, below) sacked it in 1316. At nearby Ardscull he defeated the Earl of Carrick and Lord Offaly, Sir Edmund Butler and John FitzGerald, respectively.

T*h*e GERALDINES

The term Geraldine (Gearaltach) was a euphemism for branches of the FitzGerald family in Desmond and in Kildare. They were often called Gréagaigh (Greeks) in Irish poetry because some believed that the family originated in Greece. There are also suggestions of their having

Italian origins, from the same stock as the noble Gherardini. Thomas
Davis (1814–1845) accepted Florentine influence as well as actions in
France and in the Crusades in his poem 'The Geraldines':

> The Geraldines! The Geraldines!—'tis full a thousand years
> Since, 'mid the Tuscan vineyards, bright flashed their battle-spears;
> When Capet seized the crown of France, their iron shields were known
> And their sabre-dint struck terror on the banks of the Garonne;
> Across the downs of Hastings they spurred hard by William's side
> And the grey sands of Palestine with Moslem blood they dyed;
> But never then, nor thence till now has falsehood or disgrace
> Been seen to soil FitzGerald's plume, or mantle in his face . . .

Davis tells 'how royally [they] reigned 'o'er . . . rich Kildare and English
arts disdained', then:

> What gorgeous shrines, what Brehon lore, what minstrel feasts there were
> In and around Maynooth's grey keep, and palace-filled Adare!
> But not for rite or feast ye stayed when friend or kin were pressed,
> And foemen fled when 'Crom Abú' bespoke your lance in rest.
>
> Ye Geraldines! Ye Geraldines, since Silken Thomas flung
> King Henry's sword on council board, the English thanes among,
> Ye never ceased to battle brave against the English sway,
> Though axe and brand and treachery, your proudest cut away . . .'

Maurice FitzGerald (above) who had helped Dermot MacMurrough
recover Leinster, was the progenitor of the Geraldines who became
Ireland's most powerful dynasty for seven centuries (he and other Anglo-
Normans were rebels who regarded themselves as gentlemen of blood).
Some of them became attached to the Irish, but Maurice was pragmatic
enough to say 'We are Englishmen to the Irish and Irishmen to the
English'. Over the seven centuries, the Kildare Geraldines occupied most
of the county and portions of Dublin, Carlow, Offaly and Laois. They
acquired additional properties, mainly castles, across Ireland. Astutely,
they intermarried with influential families in England and Ireland.

The Irish saying 'They lost the run of themselves' applied to some; the
early Geraldines exacted harsh tributes on citizens and abused their
power considerably. Barons of the King, they spoke English and
observed English customs and etiquette.

Gerald FitzMaurice FitzGerald (d.c. 1205), Maurice's second son, was created First Baron of Offaly at Maynooth shortly before his death. His son, Maurice FitzGerald II (c. 1194–1257) the Second Baron of Offaly was Justiciar from 1232–45. He led an attack in 1234 on Richard Marshal, Earl of Pembroke and Lord of Leinster, at the Curragh in which Marshal lost his life. Maurice then set out with Richard de Burgh (d. 1243) to conquer Connaught. They succeeded but failed to press their advantage towards Donegal and Fermanagh. Maurice arrived late to fight for King Henry III in Wales in 1245 and lost the judiciarship as a result. He founded a Franciscan monastery in Youghal c. 1235 where, after more fighting on the continent, he became a member of the community and later died there.

ENTER SCOTLAND — BRIEFLY

After defeating England at Bannockburn in 1314, the Scottish king, Robert Bruce (1274–1329), attempted to secure Irish allies to join with the Welsh and Scots against England. Gaelic chieftains welcomed the arrival of Robert's brother Edward in 1315 and his self-appointment as King of Ireland (c. 1 May 1316. See Baronies, above). They saw it as a positive step towards re-establishing the High Kingship that they wanted for themselves. King Robert followed and the pair gathered a large army. For three years they generated disorder as they attempted to drive out the Anglo-Norman settlers. Kildare castle withstood Edward's siege in the winter of 1315/16 and the town passed into the possession of the FitzGerald family. Edward was luckier at Athy where he defeated the English army under the 'Earl of Karryk', Edmund Butler (d. 1321).

Edward fell at the battle of Faughart, Co. Louth in 1318, so ending the pseudo-High-Kingship and hopes of a Gaelic revival. One of many efforts to thwart the Bruces' anti-Norman campaign here was King Edward II's (1282–1387) formal installation of John FitzThomas FitzGerald (d. 1316), Sixth Baron of Offaly (seventh by tenure) as First Earl of Kildare shortly before his death.

The achievement of arms of the Earls of Kildare includes an ape. The story goes that when the first earl was a baby, a tamed ape rescued him from his cradle during a fire in his father's castle at Woodstock, Athy. Carrying the infant to the battlements, the ape made pretences of tossing the child to the ground, to the consternation of his parents and the household gathered below. But he held the child safely until the fire burnt out. The incident inspired the nickname (Fitz)Thomas the Ape–(In Irish and Latin, Tomás an Apa and Tomas Simiacus).

Thomas FitzGerald, the Second Earl of Kildare was Lord Lieutenant from 1327 to 1328. Maurice FitzThomas FitzGerald, the Third Earl and Maurice FitzGerald the Fourth Earl were not unduly prominent (the latter was imprisoned in Dublin Castle in 1345 and 1346). Gerald FitzGerald, the Fifth Earl of Kildare (d. 1410) had only one legitimate child, Elizabeth (alias Joan). In 1432 she married the widowed 'White Earl', James Butler, the Fourth Earl of Ormond (c. 1390–1452). This gave Ormond ownership of a considerable portion of FitzGerald lands and dissipated their wealth.

In 1426, John Cam (Crooked) FitzGerald, the Sixth Earl of Kildare (d. 1427) enlarged Maynooth Castle. Thomas FitzMaurice FitzGerald (d. 1478) was the Seventh Earl of Kildare and he re-consolidated the Geraldine position by supporting the Yorkists in the War of the Roses (1455–87) and by repossessing lost estates, particularly from the Ormond Butlers.

The FitzGeralds remained powerful into the sixteenth century, when the family was at its most influential, (see The Geraldines Again. Chapter 5) and the name continues into the modern period (see Chapters 6 and 7).

OTHER NORMAN INFLUENCES

There were other Anglo-Norman influences in Co. Kildare. A Robert de Veal (sometimes le Veal or Calf. An effigy in Timolin churchyard was said to represent him), Lord of Saint Fagan's, Llandaff, came with Strongbow and received lands in Timolin, while Walter de Veele (d. 1333) became bishop of Kildare in 1300. In 1310, during his episcopacy, Kildare town hosted a sitting of parliament.

The first stone castle was built in Kildare in the early thirteenth century by the Earl Marshal on the site of the present castle. Also at this time Kildare cathedral and abbey were restored. Being a frontier town of the Pale (see The Pale, Chapter 5), Kildare was subject to raids by the dispossessed native Irish.

There was further shiring of Kildare in 1345, but the Offelan Geraldines were still by far the most influential forces in the region. The

Earl of Kildare was arrested and held in Dublin Castle between 1345 and 1346. Sir Edward FitzEustace was Lord Deputy of Ireland in the 1400s while his son, Sir Roland from Harristown, was Lord Treasurer and Lord Deputy. During that period a General Council (1415) and a Great Council (1426) assembled at Naas. Sir Roland founded a Franciscan Observantine friary in Kilcullen c. 1486. The Anglo-Normans settled too at Ardree, near Athy and built a motte at Dunboris. Because their safety required permanent defences in these troubled times, they set about building the Pale.

RAMPARTS, REBELLIONS *and* RAIDERS

T*he* PALE

MANY CAMBRO OR ANGLO-NORMAN SETTLERS inter-married and became '*Hibernis ipsis Hiberniores*' or more Irish than the Irish themselves. At the opening of the fifteenth century, therefore, English domination had weakened to the extent that its Dublin-centred control began concentrating on what the establishment referred to as four obedient counties: Louth, Meath[1], Dublin and Kildare. Eventually they would be contained within a double ditch six feet in depth, leaving a rampart close to the width of a cart between them. It was almost a century later, however, that it became known as The Pale, from the Latin word *palus* meaning a stake or boundary (a 1446 use of the term was proven to be a later addendum). The course of the 'English Pale' altered over time; the original line curving from Dundalk through Athboy, but later (1515) running through Ardee, Kells and Dangan to enter Co. Kildare at Kilcock. Later still there was a reduction in the area it enclosed and by 1537 its northern boundary had fallen from Dundalk to Drogheda. Around Mainham and Clongowes Wood, traces remain of the earlier line that it took in the direction of Clane. Continuing through Naas and Kilcullen it swung sharply and ran towards Ballymore Eustace, then back through Rathmore. It entered Co. Dublin at Rathcoole and continued through Tallaght to the coast at Dalkey.

The Bishop of Kildare and the County Sheriff were empowered to force landowners to construct the ditch. The political situation sometimes demanded the extension of its boundaries as far as the River Barrow. This led to the saying 'They dwelt beyond the law who dwelt west of the Barrow'. That law ordained that Co. Kildare should remain under the jurisdiction of the Dublin government which until about 1509 had governed it as a normal English shire. It had a royal sheriff, a chief serjeant, sub-serjeants, chief justices, justices, officials for confiscating property and lesser administrators.

The building of tower houses to defend the Pale may have begun c. 1414, when Sir John Talbot ('Scourge of France' c. 1387–1453), was the King's Lieutenant in Ireland. He arrived in Ireland in 1414 and Naas hosted a council the following year. Talbot repaired the Barrow crossing in Athy and added new fortification. In 1420, James FitzGerald, Sixth Earl of Desmond ('The Usurper'. d. 1462) slaughtered a large contingent of the O'More army at the Red Moor near Athy and inspired the folk tradition that the sun stood still in the sky for three hours to facilitate the devastation (see Wizards and Spectres, below).

Richard, Duke of York, came to Ireland as Lieutenant in 1449. In 1454, John Mey (d. 1456), the Archbishop of Armagh, sent a report to him on behalf of the Earl of Ormond which complained of:

> . . . a variance betwixt therle of Wilteshire lieutenante of this said land and Thomas Fitzxmorice of the Geraldynes for the tirle and manners of Maynoth and Rathmore in the counte of Kildare which hath caused more destruccionne in . . . Kildare and liberte of Mith within short tyme now late passed and daily doth, then was done by Irish enemys and English reblles of long time before.[2]

The report told how these enemies and rebels entered Co. Kildare, burning towns and churches, taking prisoners and looting and how the Earl of Ormond's cousin, William Butler, destroyed the 'dayly sustenaunce' of the city of Dublin'. In the same year, the Irish Council appointed Thomas FitzMaurice FitzGerald, Seventh Earl of Kildare, as Governor of Ireland. He held the office almost continuously until 1478 and was also appointed Lord Justice in 1460. Thomas directed the Irish government and held two sittings of parliament in Naas in 1456 and

1461. In 1460, Irish legislation came under imperial control but acts passed by the Irish Parliament would still be binding in Ireland. Up to its fall from grace in 1534, the House of Kildare governed the country. During that period, they used their power to seize lands of absentee landlords and use their accruing tithes and profits for themselves.

A 1465 Act demanded that:

> *Every Irish man dwelling among the English in the counties of Dublin, Meath, Uriel [meaning the Louth portion of Oriel within The Pale], or Kildare shall go like an Englishman in apparel, and shaving of his beard above the mouth, and shall within one year take to him an English name of one town as Sutton, Chester, Trym, Cork, Kinsale, or colour as white, black, brown, or art or sciences as smith, carpenter, or office as cook, butler, and he and his issue shall use this name under penalty of forfeiting his goods yearly till the aforesaid be done, to be levied two times by year for the King's wars.*[3]

An earlier (1429) Act had offered subsidies of £10 towards building fortified castles in counties Louth, Meath, Dublin and Kildare, but a 1472 parliament at Naas ordered the imposition of the same levy throughout Co. Kildare towards the construction of two castles. One was at Windgates, near Celbridge, and another near Naas. They strengthened the existing line of fortifications at Naas, Blackhall, Clongowes Wood, Rathcoffey and Maynooth. Alongside these Kildare castles, 'fenced houses' were constructed and walled bawns protected cattle against raiders from without The Pale. In 1474, Thomas FitzMaurice FitzGerald was instrumental in establishing the Fraternity (Guild) of Saint George for the defence of The Pale.

The tower houses of The Pale in Co. Kildare were mostly semi-circular or square while Co. Meath's were circular. Larger examples were turreted.

T*h*e GERALDINES AGAIN

At the height of their power, between 1470 and 1534, the Earls of Kildare were claiming authority over a subservient parliament. Although formally the King's principal representatives in Ireland, they patronised Gaelic bards, seanchaíthe and scholars, offering them hospitality in their gracious homes. The *Red Book of Kildare*, compiled in Latin, bears a frontispiece in English that reads:

Memorandum that this Boke was begon in the yere of our lord God MCCCCCIII [1503], or this at leynth. A thousynd fyve hundered & thre, by the right noble Lorde Gerald fitzThomas, Erle of Kildare As herafter the Contentes of the same more pleyne doth Appiere. Whiche was copied out of his Evidences.[4]

The frontispiece was referring to 'Gearóid Mór', Gerald (Garrett) FitzGerald (1456–1513), the Eighth Earl of Kildare, also known as the 'Great Earl'. To compile the work that contained vital historical information, he engaged Philip Flattisbury (c. 1470–1530) from Johnstown, near Kill, whom he considered 'a worthie gentleman and diligent antiquarie.' Begun in around 1503, it listed royalty, nobles and bishops and contained assorted documents, including the title deeds of FitzGerald properties. After the rebellion of Silken Thomas (see below) and the forfeiture of his estates, Tudor agents attempted to seize the Red Book but failed and it remained in family hands.

Garrett's skill at manipulating royalty consolidated his appointment as Governor (Lord Deputy) of Ireland, a position he held for all but three years between 1478 and 1513. To secure his territories, he managed to persuade King Henry VII (1457–1509) to introduce an Act of Parliament appointing the County Assizes to be held at Naas and Athy, an arrangement that remained in force until 1859 when Athy lost its Assizes. He supported the Yorkist pretender to the throne, Lambert Simnel (c. 1475–1535), and ratified his 1487 coronation in Dublin as Edward VI.[5] Simnel landed 2,000 German mercenaries in Lancashire to pursue his ambition but was defeated at Stoke Field. When he finally reached the royal palace, it was not as king but as a kitchen hand! This exercise of autonomy was the main reason for the enactment of Poynings' Law, by which Sir Edward Poynings (1459–1521; Lord Deputy 1494–95) obliged the Irish parliament to obtain approval from the king and Privy Council to hold sessions of parliament and propose draft legislation.

In 1495 Garrett burned the church in Cashel. Henry VII sought an explanation and Garrett cynically stated that he thought the Archbishop was inside. Advisers told the king that all Ireland could not govern Garrett and Henry VII is alleged to have retorted 'Then, let him govern all Ireland'. Through judicious marriages, lines of blood relationships extended his influence among the great Irish families, including the O'Neills of Tyrone. He and his Co. Kildare retainers allied with a force from Dublin and others within The Pale in an assault on Connaught on 19 August 1504. Chieftains like the Burkes, O'Donnells, O'Neills,

O'Reillys and O'Connors, some from within Connaught, supported him. Garrett's son-in-law, Ulick Burke (de Burgh) of Clanrickard led the Connaught force that had the support of O'Brien of Thomond, O'Kennedy, O'Carroll and MacNamara of Ely and others. The battle took place at Knockdoe, Co. Galway. There were some 2,000 casualties from the 10,000 participants in what was, arguably, the biggest battle that ever took place between Irish axemen. King Henry VII (1487–1509) rewarded Garrett's victory by making him a Knight of the Garter.

After Garrett's death from a gunshot wound, his son Gearóid Óg FitzGerald (Young Garrett, 1487–1534), the Ninth Earl, became Governor (1513). He commissioned Philip Flattisbury to write the *Annals of Ireland*. It complemented the earlier chronicles of Giraldus Cambrensis. Gearóid Óg was a cousin of Henry VIII (1491–1547). He continued his father's project of collecting a library of scholarly works and manuscripts in Latin, English and French in Maynooth Castle which, during his tenure, became one of the country's most opulent. He campaigned against the O'Reillys and the O'Mores and pursued a policy of Irish unity, of 'Ireland for the Irish'. In 1515, Gearóid received a grant of two charters for the towns of Kildare and Athy and privileges in respect of Maynooth and Ardmullen.

He leased portions of his estates to Gaelic activists and established the College of Saint Mary near his castle in Maynooth. His father's will had provided for the building of the college on 491 acres of his property. Gearóid Óg established the college under a 1518 licence from William Rokeby (d.c. 1523), Archbishop of Dublin. Part of this college later became a Church of Ireland church.

In 1525 he ordered the flogging of those associated with the killing of the Bishop of Leighlin, Maurice Doran. Among his retainers were harpers and rhymers, including Owen Keynan of Cappervarget, near Rathangan, who later incited a revolt in Offaly in 1539.

Gearóid was summoned to England in 1519 and lost his appointment as Lord Deputy in 1520 due to alleged 'seditious practices, conspiracies and subtle drifts'. He was forced to remain in the London area until his return from England in 1523.

During subsequent terms as Lord Lieutenant (1524–28) and (1532–34) he began facing opposition within the Pale and Leinster, particularly in disputes about coyne and livery. Gearóid especially resented the appointment of Sir William Skeffington (1467–1535) as

Special King's Commissioner in Ireland in 1529 and as Lord Lieutenant in 1530. Skeffington assembled the Irish Parliament in 1531 in an attempt to control Kildare and other Irish lords by enacting stiffer laws. By refusing to cooperate Gearóid thwarted his efforts and, the following year, succeeded in persuading Henry VIII to reinstate him as Lord Lieutenant. Concern about his position prompted him to transfer some ordnance from Dublin Castle to his own bailiwick in 1553. In the face of such intransigence, Skeffington was re-instated and Gearóid was summoned to London c. September 1533. Accused of disloyalty to the Crown, he was incarcerated in the Tower of London, where he died, it was said, of a broken heart.

Gearóid's daughter from his second marriage to Lady Grey (b.c. 1461), his second Countess, was Lady Elizabeth FitzGerald. She was the 'Fair Geraldine' immortalised in the love poems of Henry Howard (c. 1517–1547) Earl of Surrey and Lord Lieutenant of Ireland (1520–21). She was sister of the 'Wizard Earl' (see below) and half-sister of Thomas FitzGerald (1513–1537), the Tenth Earl of Kildare. Because of fringes on the helmets worn by his retainers, he became better known by his soubriquet 'Silken Thomas'.

T*b*e KILDARE REBELLION

The Kildare rebellion of 1534 to 1535 was exacerbated by the unstable situation of the period, by reaction to Geraldine policy and to the policies of centralisation being exercised by King Henry VIII. It was sparked off, however, by Gearóid Óg's appointing Silken Thomas as Deputy Governor of Ireland before his own forced departure for London. At a meeting of the Irish Privy Council at Saint Mary's Abbey, Dublin, in June 1534, this dashing young Geraldine denounced government policies, renounced allegiance to the King of England and proclaimed a Catholic crusade. Many sources cite unfounded rumours of his father's execution as a reason for Thomas's reaction, but others state that Gearóid Óg succeeded in informing his son of his maltreatment and that this exacerbated his fury.

Silken Thomas initiated the Kildare Rebellion by seizing Dublin. In July 1534, his supporters murdered the city's Archbishop (John Alen, 1476–1534). Thomas then fought a spirited campaign that ended when

Sir William Skeffington, again Lord Lieutenant, attacked Maynooth Castle in 1535, using siege guns. Thomas was away gathering reinforcements and his constable, one Christopher Paris, agreed to Skeffington's offer of money to betray his master. But when Skeffington took the castle he executed Paris and his men in what Kildare people drolly called the 'Pardon of Maynooth'. Skeffington then conducted a roundup of FitzGeralds. He sent Silken Thomas and five uncles to their deaths by execution at Tyburn, London in February 1537.

WIZARDS AND SPECTRES

The half brother of Silken Thomas, the Eleventh 'Wizard Earl', Gearóid Óg FitzGerald (c. 1525–1585) was then a twelve-year-old minor. Because he was the male who would perpetuate the Geraldine dynasty, his loyal supporters went to great lengths to protect him. They smuggled him out of Ireland and, after moving from one place of refuge to another, he received his education in Rome. He served for a time as Master of the Horse in the service of the Duke of Florence. When Henry VIII died in 1547 and Edward VI succeeded him, Gearóid returned to England where he met and married Mabel, the daughter of Sir Antony Browne K.G. who interceded with Edward and had the Irish FitzGerald estates restored to Gearóid c. 1552. Gearóid came back to Kilkea, near Athy. A passionate preoccupation with alchemy earned him his soubriquet and a considerable amount of notoriety. Folk tradition tells how, every seven years, his mounted ghost emerges from the Rath of Mullamast and gallops to and around the Curragh before returning to occupy a haunted room in Kilkea Castle. He will continue this ritual until the horse's silver shoes wear out. Then he and his army will sleep inside the Rath of Mullamast, waiting to emerge and free Ireland some day (see Chapter 9).

The FitzGeralds had properties and appointments in over thirty Kildare townlands. In the main, the family was respectable and respected. Inevitably, however, there was an occasional scandal. A vicar of Kilmeague, Pierse FitzGerald, kept Catherine O'Rourke, the daughter of his predecessor, as a concubine. Richard FitzGerald of Kilteel had one illegitimate son by the daughter of a neighbour and another by a prostitute whom he kept. With the help of his sons, Walter Reagh FitzGerald, the son-in-law of Fiach MacHugh O'Byrne, killed the family of the Sheriff of Kildare in Athy in March 1594. He was hanged in chains the following March.

The FitzGeralds also had their eccentrics. The Countess of Desmond, for example, married the Twelfth Earl of Kildare (d. 1597). Tradition states that she died after falling from a cherry tree aged 140, but historians place her age at 100 years, sometimes less (c. 1545–1638).

The merciless crushing of the Silken Thomas rebellion ended the supremacy of the house of Kildare. With the family's hereditary viceroyalty gone, English control over Ireland tightened. Indeed, the execution of seven senior Geraldines and the confiscation of their Maynooth seat affected the county's entire population. It also signalled a phase of significant change in the political, economic, religious and social climate by which Co. Kildare would suffer the oppressions of the complex, multi-faceted Reformation. These included the suppression of monastic houses.

In time, the diocese of Kildare became impoverished and, up to the mid-sixteenth century, its bishops sold off properties to survive. The establishment confiscated important monastic settlements at Athy, Castledermot, Kildare, Naas and Clane. They were used as strategic strongholds or bestowed as rewards on officials and military men who had been prominent in crushing the rebellion.

The conflict brought about the destruction of property on a massive scale and encouraged enemy septs from outside the county boundaries—the O'Mores, O'Tooles, O'Connors and Kavanaghs—to raid.

Like Co. Kildare, Ireland suffered. From then on, a Viceroy from England would represent the monarch in Ireland and there would be an English army in the country—in all thirty-two counties until 1922 and in the six north-eastern counties to date.

PLANTATION

The Tudor conquest of Ireland took place during the reigns of four sovereigns. Henry VIII became King of England in 1509 and an Irish Act of Parliament made him King of Ireland in 1541. Edward VI (1547–53), Mary I (1516–58) and Elizabeth I (1533–1603) followed.

The sixteenth century saw Kildare's loyal gentry representing the county in the Irish Parliament: Aylmers, Berminghams, Eustaces, Suttons, Wellesleys and Wogans. These and other less aristocratic families (Archibalds, Drugans, Flattisburys, Keatings, Kellys, Kerdiffs, Walshs, Sexs and Sherlocks) administered justice and organised defence in their local areas, particularly along the county's western and southern boundaries.

At the dawn of the seventeenth century English power was largely confined to the area within the Pale. This posed a threat to England, since enemies like Catholic Spain could occupy and use the vast Irish-governed remainder of Ireland to launch an invasion. The Tudor monarchs, therefore, and the Stuart king, James I (1566–1625) in particular, devised and initiated a policy of 'plantation'. In their way of thinking, the concept envisaged supplanting the indolent Irish with industrious English and Scottish settlers who would promote a civilised, God-fearing way of life by their example. It overlooked the fact that the new arrivals would need the services of the native Irish, would inter-marry with or suffer harassment from a deprived people and might—God between us and all harm—become 'more Irish than the Irish themselves'.

The first Tudor attempts at implementing the concept outside the borders of The Pale in King's County and Queen's County (Offaly and Laois) took place between 1549 and 1556. Arrangements became more permanent there after 1563. This was the territory of the O'Mores and O'Connors and the implementation was not without problems; the administration of the two counties was costing twenty times more than the revenue they were yielding.

Another problem was affecting Co. Kildare people. The *Annals of the Four Masters* records that in the Age of Christ 1575, Naas was among the places affected by a plague caused by intense heat:

> *. . . there was no rain for one hour, by night or day from Bealtaine to Lammas. A loathsome disease and a dreadful malady . . . raged virulently among the Irish and English . . . in Naas of Leinster . . . many a castle was left without a guard, many a flock without a shepherd, and many a noble corpse without burial, in consequence of this distemper.*

Plans for the plantation of six Ulster counties emerged in 1609–1610. By 1641 over 15,000 Scots and English had settled in Ulster and 22,000 English in Munster.

MORE REBELLION

The Ulster Plantation was the most comprehensive and also suffered most from the rebellion of 1641, which might have succeeded but for a drunken episode revealing plans to seize Dublin Castle. From it developed the Confederate War of 1641–53, also known as the War of the Confederation, the Eleven Years War or the Irish Civil War. Civil War (1642–46) in England exacerbated an already confused situation. It was a religion-driven crisis of subjects against the monarchy.

The government proclaimed the rebellion 'a conspiracy intended by some evil-affected Irish papists' but quickly made it clear that they 'did not intend or mean any of the Old English lords of the Pale . . . we being well assured of their fidelity to the Crown.' Thomas Carlyle (1795–1881) later wrote:

> There [were] Catholics of the Pale demanding freedom of religion under my Lord this and my Lord that. There [were] old Irish Catholics under Pope's Nuncios . . . and Owen Roe O'Neill [c. 1582–1649, see below] demanding, not religious freedom only but what we now call Repeal of the Union, and unable to agree with Catholics of the English Pale.[6]

During the confused years of strife, mainly involving Ulster Irish opposition to English rule and to the policy of plantation, an estimated 35,000 English fell. On behalf of the English settlers, the Earl of Kildare raised and armed three companies. However, word spread of Rory O'More's (d. 1652) defeat of government forces at Julianstown, near Drogheda, on 29 November 1641 and of subsequent brutalities in Co. Wicklow, and so most of the newly-equipped forces deserted with their weapons. Many of these were Old English gentlemen of The Pale who were disgruntled at concessions earlier offered by Charles I (1600–1649; King of Britain and Ireland 1625–49) remaining unratified. They hid out around Celbridge and Naas.

A gate in Athy's fortifications was called after Thomas Preston (1585–1655), then the Confederate Catholic Commander-in-Chief. The Earl of Castlehaven and Derby, James Touchet (Lord Audley, d. 1631) was General of his Leinster Horse. In 1631, Castlehaven conducted a bombardment of Kildare town that destroyed its garrison and cathedral. After the attack, the town was described as being nearly uninhabited.

James Butler (1610–1688), the Twelfth Earl of Ormond (later First Duke), was acting Commander-in-Chief of Crown forces. On 1 February 1642, he brought 2,000 infantrymen, 300 cavalry troopers and five small field guns to Naas, burning out Lyons on 31 January en route. During a two-day occupation, Ormond deployed forces that burned villages and ravaged estates, including Castlemartin at Kilcullen.

The citizens of Naas were sympathetic to the rebels, so Ormond allowed his troops to plunder the town. Because it offered good defensive features, he disobeyed orders to burn Naas, instead leaving a garrison behind. He took a local Franciscan, Father Higgins, back to Dublin, allegedly for protection from the garrison, Ormond claimed, because the man had supported English deserters of the area. A bloodthirsty Governor of Dublin, Sir Charles Coote, seized the unfortunate cleric and hanged him. The following year, Ormond held Athy against the Confederate Catholics but Owen Roe O'Neill (who had returned from the continent in 1642 and had replaced Sir Phelim O'Neill [c. 1606–1653] as the Ulster Irish General the following year) re-captured the town in 1645 and occupied Rheban Castle.

Whenever possible, however, Ormond was inclined to make terms because he envisaged eventually receiving Irish help in what he considered an inevitable final heave against English rule. Meanwhile, provisions were unobtainable in Naas, even to its garrison.

The country's Lord Justices further fanned the flames of revolution when they charged people of quality, even some who had not joined in the rebellion, with high treason. There were 300 such cases in February 1642 alone. In April 1642, Ormond returned with a larger force and burned the property of rebels throughout the county. He defeated Viscount Mountgarrett and Rory O'Moore at Kilrush on 15 April and received a gem worth £500 from the English Parliament for his achievements.

He placed a Lieutenant Colonel Gibson in charge of a reinforced garrison in Naas, then installed a new Sovereign and eight burgesses.

While landowners continued their rebellion, a small garrison, called a custodium, secured each vacated estate. In 1643, these, and Naas itself with a garrison of 1,000 now under Sir Arthur Loftus, suffered during the continuing shortage of provisions. Troops were almost naked, and starving. Sir Frank Huncks, Governor, said they raised the pity of everyone who saw them. Something had to be done, so, at the behest of the Lord Justices, Ormond met the Irish Commissioners at Jigginstown, Naas, in August and a cessation of hostilities followed. Ormond became Lord Lieutenant in November 1643 and was formally sworn in on 21 January 1644. Two years later he passed through Kildare on his way to Kilkenny. Rebels still continuing the struggle in Kildare planned to attack him but he learned of their intentions and made good his escape.

A few weeks later, Preston was threatening Ormond's Dublin stronghold and made an expedition into Kildare, where he burned mills and crops and destroyed bridges.

By 1647, Ormond realised he could no longer hold Ireland for the Crown. He surrendered Dublin to the Parliament whereupon Preston moved to occupy English-held garrisons. He took Naas and surrounding garrisons but later abandoned and burned them. Ormond was back with reinforcements the following year, again as Lord Lieutenant, when he took Allen and Naas. Then a sinister cloud darkened the Irish landscape. An impressive navy, a substantial artillery train and a force of 20,000 backed the man who would become notorious for his fierce campaign in Ireland–Oliver Cromwell (1600–1658).

CROMWELL

In 1649, the English Civil War ended with the trial and execution of Charles I (1600–1649). Parliament abolished the monarchy and dispatched Oliver Cromwell and his puritan army to conquer the Irish and exact revenge for disloyalty, for the massacre of Protestants at Portadown Bridge and for the only pitched battle ever won by the Gaelic Irish at Benburb (1646). The well-remembered slogan 'To Hell or to Connaught' ignored the fact that Co. Clare also received some of the native Irish and Old English that Cromwell drove from prime lands in the remaining twenty-six counties. A subordinate, Hewson, marched from Dublin. He took Naas and Athy and occupied Ballysonan in March 1650. The Moat of Ardscull was one of his fortifications. In the subsequent 'Cromwellian Settlement' the Government reserved Co. Kildare.

FINE GIRL Y'ARE

When Sir William Petty (1623–1687) was physician to the army in Ireland between 1655 and 1667, he conducted a survey of lands forfeited in 1641. Later, as Surveyor General of Ireland, he sent questionnaires to resident gentlemen. Some of the replies offer a glimpse of Kildare's mid-seventeenth century folk. Edited, an extract reads:

> The men are hardy, laborious and industrious, of healthful bodies and constitutions, able and enured to bear labour and live to a great age—generally to seventy and eighty, some to a hundred and some much longer . . . Their diet is generally very mean and sparing, consisting of milk, roots and coarse unsavoury bread; their lodging and habit proportionable. They are of good sense and easily give way to reason if plainly demonstrated and, where they have the advantage of language and education extremely improve, being silent, studious and thoughtful . . .
>
> Their women differ not much in habit from those of other countries, generally inclined to corpulency and thick-legged, which is occasioned by their loose garments, flat pumps and brogues, using little or no action or exercises, in or without their houses, having easy labour and being good nurses but bad house-wives, not being used to any sort of manual labour except spinning, which by reason of the suppleness of their fingers they perform well.
>
> They are great admirers of music, yet their own songs generally are doleful lamentations as those of a conquered people . . .
>
> They are not very lascivious, yet the ordinary sort of people take a sort of pride in prostituting their daughters or kinswomen to their landlord's sons or kinsmen . . . and if the young women bear a child or children, the parents are exceedingly fond of it, and the grandfather divides his estate equally to such as to the legitimate; and further, if they happen to nurse a gentleman's child, whose parents fall into decay or want, they think themselves bound to provide for that nursechild as for their own, it having drawn of the same milk.[7]

Charles II (1630–1685) was King of England and Ireland from 1660 to 1685. James II (1633–1701) succeeded him. In 1689 he lost the throne to William III (1650–1702), known as William of Orange. In an attempt to regain it by conquering Ireland, James landed at Kinsale, thus initiating the Williamite War. He failed, being beaten at the Battle of the Boyne in 1690.

MILITIA

In 1688, Catholics owned 22 per cent of Irish lands. This had dwindled to a mere seven per cent by 1714. The loss was reflected among Co. Kildare landowners. While Jonathan Swift (1667–1745) was visiting Vanessa in Celbridge (see Celbridge Abbey. Chapter 7) and 'utterly rejecting everything wearable that comes from England', Henry Grattan (1746–1820), a Protestant advocating Catholic Emancipation, was coming to prominence. He articulated demands for reform at a 1783 convention in Dublin, but they were rejected. The political preface to the French Revolution was being written and Irishmen, including prominent Kildare citizens, were reading it. The United Irishmen were emerging, and two of their leaders had strong Kildare connections. Sensing danger, landlords raised local forces of volunteers (later yeomanry).

Early Protestant militia had emerged in 1666 but had disbanded less than twenty years later. They had re-emerged for a period during the Williamite War. In 1756, Co. Kildare had two regiments totalling less than 1,000 in units raised at local level. New volunteers replaced regular troops withdrawn from the colonies to fight in the American War of Independence (1776–83). Kildare units included Athy Carabiniers, Athy Independents, Athy Light Dragoons, Athy Rangers and Independent Volunteers, Athy Volunteers, Carton Union, Castledermot Horse, Castledermot Volunteers, Castletown Union, Celbridge Volunteers, Clane Rangers (also Clane Horse or Clane Cavalry), Curragh Rangers, Kilcock Rangers, Kilcullen Rangers, Kildare Rangers (or Corps), Kildare Infantry, Kildare Volunteers, Leixlip Volunteers, Loyal Kilcock Rangers and Infantry, Maynooth Corps, Monasterevin Volunteers, Naas Independent Light Dragoons, Naas Rangers and Rathangan Union.

One unit is remembered in song:

> *Attend, ye good fellows, and lend me your ears*
> *While I sing to the praise of the Clane Volunteers;*
> *Who were summoned together by Leinster's great Duke*
> *The French to chastise and the Dons to rebuke*[8]

Protestant officers led mainly Catholic rank and file in a new Irish Militia established in 1793. This posed a moral problem for many during a historic event in which Co. Kildare played a prominent role–the rebellion of 1798.

6 'AS T*he* STORM SWEEPS DOWN ...'1798

One Rebel chastising another, named Toban, for killing a landlord named Brewer after the Battle of Prosperous:

> 'You have murdered the good man who kept us from starving.'
> Toban's reply:
> 'What he had is now in our hands, and we have saved him the trouble of being kind again.'

ALTHOUGH BEREFT of their former power, the Kildare Geraldines re-emerged politically during the eighteenth century. They were prominent in the Irish Brigade when the Regiment of FitzGerald won special renown in the War of Spanish Succession (1701–14). The Nineteenth Earl, Robert (1675–1744), was Lord Justice in 1714 when he redesigned Carton House (see Fine Houses, Chapter 7). James Edward (1722–1773) the Twentieth Earl, had disputes with the Government, yet was Lord Justice (1756–57) and Master-general of Ordnance (1758–66). He became Viscount Leinster of Taplow on 21 February 1746. On 3 March 1761 his lordship was advanced to the Marquessate of Kildare in Ireland and on 26 November 1766 he was created Duke of Leinster. The Duke's town house in Dublin (1745) is now known as Leinster House, seat of Dáil Éireann, the Irish parliament. His son, Lord Edward FitzGerald (1763–1798) was prominent in the 1798 rebellion. This major event in Irish history had its beginnings in Co. Kildare, where the strength of the United Irishmen fluctuated between 11,000 and 12,000. Their action has been the subject of a number of studies and many arguments as to accuracy. Only a few facets can be dealt with in this short volume.

Lord Edward FitzGerald (see Personalities, below), the military leader of the rebellion, was born in London but lived at Carton, Maynooth. He later lived for a while in Kildare town. Like today, Kildare shopkeepers of the time bought their goods in Dublin. They also picked up seditious material too and found the sentiments of Thomas Paine's (1737–1809) *Rights of Man* impressive. In *Some Accounts of the First Apparent Symptoms of the Late Rebellion* (Dublin, 1800) James Alexander wrote of the changing political atmosphere 'Newspapers went a good way into the business, for I never knew the people in [Co. Kildare] anything like so attached to these vehicles of information and political sentiment'. Avid readers or not, people of influence in the United Irishmen movement lived in Co. Kildare (see Personalities, below). The main areas of action were: Ballitore, Ballymore Eustace, Clane, Crookstown, Gibbet Rath, Kilcock, Kilcullen, Kildare, Kilkea, Maynooth, Monasterevin, Naas, Narraghmore, Ovidstown, Prosperous, Rathangan and Timahoe.

NORTH KILDARE

The first actions of the 1798 Rebellion took place in North Kildare. The area's prominent liberal landlords who supported Catholic Emancipation included the Second Duke of Leinster (1780–1803) in Maynooth, Wogan Browne (1758–1812) of Castle Browne (Clongowes Wood) and Charles Aylmer (1720–1801) of Painestown House (father of William, below). A Catholic, Charles represented Co. Kildare at the Catholic 'Back Lane' Convention of 1792. Initially supportive, but later more lukewarm or conservative, were Sir Fenton Aylmer (1768–1816), Seventh Baronet of Donadea, and Michael Aylmer (c. 1750–1830) of Courtown House. Firmly belonging to the Society of United Irishmen was its prominent leader Theobald Wolfe Tone (1791–1828) a Dubliner of a Blackhall, Clane family (see Personalities, below). Archibold Hamilton Rowan (1751–1834) was another. He had been living in Rathcoffey for fourteen years before 1798 (see Personalities, below).

PROSPEROUS

The first insurgent action was successful. It took place at Prosperous during the night of 23–24 May 1798. A cotton mill in the village had failed during the previous decade, leaving a high rate of unemployed young men. About forty members of the Royal Cork City Regiment of Militia (often confused with the North Cork Militia) under Captain Swayne (d. 1798) and a Lieutenant and twenty Ancient Brittons cavalrymen (Welsh Fencibles stationed in Ireland) occupied one permanent and one temporary barracks. Swayne enlisted the aid of the clergy and an influential local doctor, John Esmonde (c. 1760–1798, see Personalities of the Rebellion, below), in an attempt to persuade the local United Irishmen to hand in their arms. This failed, so Swayne began a series of brutal raids for arms. In the process he also seized farm stock and destroyed property. This alienated Esmonde, although he continued to enjoy Swayne's hospitality. The doctor was like many men of status at the time: leaders of the yeomen by day and of the United Irishmen by night. He dined and drank with Swayne on 23 May and Swayne was probably less than sober when he retired to bed in the barracks.

At about two o'clock in the morning of 24 May, the rebels, including Esmonde, under Captain Andrew Farrell of Blackhall, Clane, attacked and killed two sentries and gained access to the sleeping quarters of the barracks. They numbered 500, according to one contemporary account. They killed Swayne in his bed, took out his body and burned it in a barrel of tar before being surprised by other soldiers who awoke and routed them. Two or three of the rebels were killed, but their comrades surrounded the barracks and set it alight with straw and bushes. A local woman, Ruth Hackett, played a heroic role carrying furze bushes for the fire from the bog nearby before being shot dead. The garrison appealed for and received the safe release of wives and children. Then the soldiers all moved upstairs but the flames reached them and they threw themselves out the window, many landing on the rebels' pikes. A fierce fight developed and most of the garrison was wiped out. A rebel prisoner being held in custody was rescued.

Yeomanry reprisals during the course of the day that followed included the burning of Staplestown church, across the bog from Prosperous (some accounts say the church was in Prosperous).

A sworn statement made by a Prosperous citizen, which, unedited, reads:

The examns. Of James
Jourdan of Prosperous in the Co. Kildare,

Weaver, who been duely sworn & examined on oath saith that he was in the town of Prosperous about the hour of three or four o'clock of Thursday morning the 24th day of May inst or at day break where he saw sevll. Bodys of his Majesty's regiment of the City of Cork militia [sic] and Antient Brittons lying dead in the street of Prosperous and at the same time this examinant sayth he saw the sevll. Persons following with arms in their hands, parading and exulting and who he verily belvs. Were the persons aided and assisted by others unknown to exat who murdered and assassinated the soldiers who examinant saw dead to witt George Fane of Cork—Fox—& Fox sons to John Fox of Healy Bridge or Newtown—Poor of the same place Patrick Farrel Michl Leeson James Tobin Denis Killy Christr Buggel Robt Hooks &—Courtney all of Prosperous aforesd. Laurence Grannam of Timahoe Michl. Huges Henry Hugges of Staplestown & Helys Bridge John McManus of Killybegs Edwd Hanlon Donore—Fleming Peter French of Blackwood turf men (?) or labourers & Andrew Farrell son to Daniel Farrell of Helys Bridge who told examt. He should have his hands in blood. This examinant sayth the above named persons aided and assisted by sevll. Others murdered and assassinated the sevll. Soldiers who were on sd. Morning murdered &c Jas Jordan

Sworn before me this 27th May 1798
Roger North

I acknowledge to be bound to our
Sovereign Ld. The King in the sum
Of 500 to prosecute when called
On or at next assizes

Jas Jordan[1]

The Battle of Prosperous is recalled too in a ballad that begins:

The chapel bell at Prosperous was pealing loud and high;
The weavers and the artisans in groups have gathered nigh,
From Blackwood and from Downings, from Longtown and Donore;
From Curryhills and Landenstown, those sturdy peasants pour;
And matrons from near Mylerstown and maids from Currabell;
The dread doings of those Yeomen in shuddering horror tell;
For those monsters of oppression and dark dishonour reign,
In that district long abandoned to the tyrant rule of Swayne.[2]

CLANE

Two officers led fifty men of the Armagh Militia who were in billets in Clane. A respected Protestant, Richard Griffith (1784–1878) of Millicent, commanded the Clane Yeoman Cavalry, many of whom were his Roman Catholic tenants. Andrew Farrell, who had led the attack on Prosperous, was one. Doctor John Esmonde, also active at Prosperous, was one of its subalterns. A Captain Jephson was in overall command. A rebel attack on Clane followed shortly after the Prosperous success. The attackers swarmed into the main street wielding pikes, sickles, scythes, pitchforks and a few blunderbusses and flintlocks. A watchful drummer spotted them but they prevented him from alerting the garrison. A bugler escaped, however, and blew reveille. The rebels seemed to know the exact houses that provided billets and it is most likely that a sympathetic yeoman named James Tierney had passed on the intelligence.

The covering fire of a garrison carbine assisted the defenders in repelling the attackers and capturing six of them. Two militiamen were killed and five seriously injured.

Dressed in Ancient Brittons uniforms captured in Prosperous, a handful of rebels later mounted horses and approached the town. Captain Jepheson met them on the Capdoo commons and the rebels faced volleys of gunfire and Jephson shot one who was attempting to strike him down. The remaining rebels retreated and hid out in friendly houses around Capdoo commons; houses that the pursuing garrison later burned. Despite his success, Griffith decided to withdraw to Naas, where he took the six prisoners. He executed one of them and had Esmond arrested for treachery.

BALLYMORE EUSTACE

A small garrison billeted in Ballymore Eustace fell to a rebel attack in the early morning of 24 May. An unknown number lost their lives and the remainder fled to Naas. A Captain Erskine passed through the town after the fight and is said to have remarked 'Neither me nor my soldiers will breakfast until we breakfast on the Croppies of Ballymore.'

NAAS

Michael Reynolds of Johnstown burned the Cork to Dublin coaches and then led a group of insurgents against Naas during the night of 23/4 May. Yeomen augmented the horse and foot soldiers that formed the garrison there. Its considerable firepower struck fear into the rebels who, despite exhortations from Reynolds, fled. Reynolds and a handful of braver souls tried to continue the fight but they too were forced to retreat, Reynolds fleeing to Co. Wicklow.

KILCULLEN

Rebels suffered defeat at Kilcullen Bridge on 24 May but on the same day Erskine attempted to discharge his personal threat (see Ballymore Eustace, above) when he led a party of Buff Dragoons past the hill of Old Kilcullen and charged some rebels who were gathered there. The rebels met him with pikes and repelled the attack. Erskine fell in a second charge.

RATHANGAN

Captain James Spencer, land agent to the Duke of Leinster, commanded the single corps of yeomanry in Rathangan. Captain Langton and a small force of South Cork Militia supported him. On 26 May, a young farmer and United Irishman, Captain John Doorley (see Personalities, below) led an attack on the town and the garrison withdrew to Naas. The Black Horse Regiment, stationed there, accompanied them back to Rathangan. The rebels had erected barricades and put up a determined defence. They repelled the counter-attack. Then the retreating attackers joined with a party of City of Cork Militia who were arriving into the area with a cannon. They availed of its firepower in a further counter-attack and dislodged the rebels.

James Spencer was a septuagenarian and a kind land agent. Many people from Rathangan and surrounding areas objected strongly to his being piked to death after the rebel's occupation. John Doorley had no part in the deed and condemned it and its perpetrators, yet his farm-house surrounded by the Bog of Allen was burned in reprisal. When the King's forces were back in command of Rathangan, they hanged a rebel, Edward Molloy of Mount Prospect, who was probably singled out because he was a former yeoman.

KNOCKAULIN

From his field headquarters in Castlemartin, General Sir Ralph Dundas, Midland Area Commander (see Personalities, below, and Fine Houses, Chapter 7), had written on 16 May to the Under-Secretary, Edward Cooke. Part of his letter had said:

> The last four days have furnished me with many very affecting scenes – my house filled with the poor deluded people, giving up their arms, receiving protections, and declaring that moment to be the happiest in their lives. Be assured that the head of the Hydra is off, and the Co. of Kildare will, for a long time, enjoy profound peace and quiet.[3]

Further flushed with optimism, Dundas received the authority of Lord Camden, Lieutenant General of Ireland, to hold a meeting at Castlemartin House, Kilcullen, with rebel representatives to discuss surrender terms. As a result of this meeting, Dundas issued a procl-amation offering a free pardon to any rebel who would, on 28 May, gather at Gibbet Rath, straddling the Dublin to Cork highway near Kildare, and surrender his arms. His action did not have the approval of his superiors but since he had promised it they supported his decision. Over 350 rebels accepted the terms and arrived at the Rath. Other rebels were already there.

GIBBET RATH

On 23 May 1798, seventeen-year-old Lieutenant William Giffard (sometimes Gifford) had been travelling on the mail coach from Limerick to Dublin. His uncle was a Limerick man, General Duff (some reports say this is incorrect, that his father was a popular militia captain, a friend of Duff's). At Kildare, rebels took Giffard from the coach and piked him.

General Duff was moving a column from Limerick to open up the route to Dublin when he heard of the atrocity. Hastening his progress, he reached Monasterevin in less than forty-eight hours of forced marching. He wrote to his Commander-in-Chief, General Lake, saying that, in order to make an example of the rebels, he was about to surround their headquarters in Kildare town with seven pieces of artillery, 150 dragoons and 350 infantryman. Then he heard about the proposed surrender at Gibbet Rath. Accompanied by a yeoman regiment and Lord Roden's Fencible Cavalry, known as 'Lord Roden's fox-hunters', he hastened to the Rath. The date was 29 May.

There are two versions of what happened next. One says that a particular rebel fired a musket in the air shouting that he had changed his mind and was refusing to surrender his weapon. Another suggests that Duff organised the discharge of a weapon to excuse what happened next. Lord Roden's Fencible Cavalry, The City of Dublin Militia, the South Cork Militia and the remainder of Duff's force charged the helpless rebels and slaughtered them. Situated as it is on the broad Curragh plain with no cover whatsoever, the carnage was complete – or almost so.

Duff submitted an account to Dublin Castle that reached the newspapers saying that when rebels fired on his troops, they retaliated. This was accepted as the official line on events at Gibbet Rath. However, a few rebels escaped by scrambling through the ranks of Duff's own troops. One, Harrington by name, was pursued but he foiled attempts at shooting him by pelting his pursuers with stones, upsetting their aim. Harrington's oral version survived. It supports the account of one man discharging a weapon, either by mistake or in a change of heart. The description of what happened next is appalling. It claims that Duff ordered the rebels to throw their arms in a pile. They did so and then he commanded them to move away from their weapons and kneel on the grass. An eerie silence descended as the rebels began to realise that they might not be going to receive the pardon promised by General Dundas after all.

Harrington passed on his account of what happened to Colonel Patrick Kelly. Kelly was a United Irishman from Kilcoo, Athy. He had been a delegate at the Castlemartin meeting (above) with Government representatives, General Dundas and General Lake when the agreement to surrender weapons was negotiated. Monasterevin yeomen involved in the massacre corroborated Harrington's statement, Kelly claimed. Kelly's summing up of the Gibbet Rath incident went:

Without ceremony, Duff commanded the rebels, as he called them, to throw their arms into a heap, and after this had been complied with, he ordered them to kneel at a distance from where the arms were thrown, saying loudly at the moment, to beg the King's pardon for the outrage of having rebelled. This command, so perfidious in its meaning and tendency, was complied with; which being done, a dead silence appeared to prevail among the troops. Major General Sir James Duff instantly thundered out, 'Charge, and spare no rebel!' Havoc, consternation and death now spread themselves on all sides. The horror of the scene was and is indescribable.

The cutting down and slaughtering of this unarmed multitude was but too easily accomplished; the troops consisted entirely of horsemen [unlikely] – the Black Horse, commanded by General Dunn, and the Foxhunters, commanded by Lord Roden, besides Capt. Bagot's yeomen cavalry, were too powerful executioners to be withstood by men who were disarmed and upon their knees. The number of victims who fell beneath these murderers' murdering sword was 325. In one street alone of Kildare town, distant from the scene of slaughter about two English miles, there were reckoned 85 widows the following morning. This carnage outweighs in enormity every act committed on either side, the army or the people, throughout the disasters of '98. The memory of it should never be effaced – it should instruct the warrior to spare, and the vanquished not to confide.

It happened now, unfortunately for the town of Kildare, that the nephew of General Sir James Duff was a passenger in the Limerick coach; and on its arrival in the town, the countrymen were scattered over part of it; and their attention was directed to see who might be inside. On discovering this young man, and finding that he was (from his own words) the nephew of a General in the army, these ill-guided men dragged him out of the coach and piked him. This circumstance alone, horrible to relate, and not to be palliated by any act of suffering or punishment inflicted on the perpetrators, might be adduced by some, in extenuation of the subsequent crime of the uncle. The dispassionate reader cannot, however, exculpate such a monster (independently of his treachery and Punic faith) for a general butchery and carnage. It was not with him, as a heathen writer advised, 'Parcere subjectis et debellare superbos.' To spare the contrite, and subdue the haughty. The people on the Rath of the Curragh of Kildare should not have been collectively immolated to appease the manes of an individual.

A few of the victims, it was said about five, escaped by running through the ranks as they were charging. A few lay as if dead, and being woefully hacked and mangled, were passed over as some of the heap of slaughtered men. One athletic young fellow ran about a mile and half, when he was pursued by eight yeomen of Bagot's corps; he gained a fallow field just adjoining the Curragh, and having so far escaped his pursuers, he stooped and picked up two stones, which he flung with such vigour against two of them, that he disabled both, and rendered them unable to discharge their pistols. Two more came on, and by a further effort, he disabled a third also, with stones which he scrambled up. It was said that two more fired at him without effect, but it was acknowledged by them that he parried the firing with so much alertness as to elude any aim they could take. The last of the yeomen assailants, who is still living in Monasterevin and whom they call Ned Cooper, received a blow of a stone from this intrepid Kildare man, in the hip, and by its effects limps and walks lame to this day. At length a dragoon, being commanded by a sanguinary officer to cut him down, the poor countryman, after all his fatigue and fighting, received a sabre wound on the neck, as he scrambled over a ditch, and fell as dead.[4]

CARBURY

A lieutenant of the Carbury Corps, Thomas Tyrrell, was High Sheriff of Co. Kildare in 1798. When rebels burned the Charter School in Carbury on 30 May, he moved his men to Clonard, across the border in Co. Meath and fortified a house there. He gave nightly shelter to the garrisons of Carbury and Johnstown Bridge. The fortified house was the scene of a significant battle in Clonard on 11 July. He beat off attacks of rebels from Wicklow, Wexford and Kildare, killing many and forcing others to return to the safety of Carbury.

KILCOCK

William Aylmer's rebels attacked and routed yeomen led by a relative, Sir Fenton Aylmer in Kilcock on 4 June (some accounts say 1 June). They burned the courthouse and barracks and later looted and burned Michael Aylmer's Courtown House before returning to their camp in Timahoe. Tommy Lube, a descendant of George Lube, wrote a ballad covering the battle and other events that occurred long after 1798 and completely unconnected with the rebellion. Tommy wrote it in Lube's public house during a visit by Val Vousden (1884–1951) to Kilcock, and the wandering actor included it in his repertoire. Part of it went:

Two centuries and fifty, aye, an old clock stands the wear,
Its printed face is faded, but it has a jewel rare
Because it holds old mem'ries, as it shakes its chants so strong,
And talks to me so knowingly, and makes me think and long.
It saw the 'Risin' proper when the 'Short Grass' glared with red,
When the pikemen of the district, in their hearts with wrongs were fed,
And they dreamed the dreams of freedom, which the world denied them long,
Then the old clock wagged its heavy weights and echoed full the song
Their fathers sung before them with Geraldine 'Abu'
And Carton Castle trembled with the wail of death and rue,
When Kildare was on its mettle and the myrmidons did mock,
That's just the tale was told me by that timepiece in Kilcock.

'Tis strange that I'd be friendly with an old clock standing there,
And yet not strange – come thinking – for my thoughts are somewhat rare
And are weighted like the timepiece with matured and ancient works
As the pendulum of homeliness wags on, and inward lurks
While the old clock grins, and winking, with its face so full of fun –
And yet of gruesome tragedy (when all is said and done)
Of '98 and Ovidstown – of the period 'Murderin' Ditch'
For when Aylmer used the mercy, 'twas old time that caused the hitch,
It came when the clock was ticking, but poor Norris died at four,
The sad old clock it told me that its works with blood did pour!
That it could not leave De-Lube's and thus save a poor wife's shock.
Thus was the tale unfolded by that timepiece in Kilcock.[5]

OVIDSTOWN

Ovidstown is close to Kilcock and when the rebels captured Maynooth on 14 June 1798, they re-grouped behind their defences in the North Kildare areas of Hortland, Newtown and Ovidstown. Some reports suggest that rebels from Meath and Wexford joined them. The intention was to advance on Dublin while the English were dealing with the troubles in Wexford. Women in the neighbourhood were busy preparing breakfast for up to 5,000 rebels under William Aylmer of Painestown, Hugh Ware of Rathcoffey and George Luby of Corcoranstown, when a regiment of Scottish Fencibles surprised them. Aylmer called on the main body of his men to fall back on Ovidstown Hill while pikemen carried out a frontal assault on enemy artillery lines.

Contrary to his orders, the pikemen attempted to encircle their objective but were cut down at a place ever since called 'The Murdering Ditch.' A ballad commemorating the event begins:

> *Oh Mary, get my coat of green,*
> *It's near the break of day,*
> *On a retreat my name shall be,*
> *It's not at home I'll stay,*
> *The ancient race unto disgrace,*
> *Shall ne'er be brought by me,*
> *Oh, I'm away to Ovidstown to fight for liberty.*
> *CHORUS*
> *With pike so keen, and sash of green,*
> *That emblem dear to me;*
> *Oh, I'm away to Ovidstown to fight for liberty.*[6]

TIMAHOE

Vinegar Hill was over, Ballinamuck too. Co. Kildare had started the action in the 1798 rebellion and, apart from Michael Dwyer's and Joseph Holt's sporadic actions in Wicklow, it was also the last to quit. In Timahoe, near Prosperous, a group of rebels, under William Aylmer, held out for four weeks after the main rebellion in the county was crushed. Aylmer had chosen his position astutely, being surrounded by bog and therefore impenetrable by cavalry. Consequently, however, it lacked adequate provisions.

A letter, dated 6 June 1798, from an Oliver Barker, Clonard, Co. Meath to John Lees, the Secretary of the Irish Post Office, tells of their distress. Unedited, it reads:

> *Sir*
>
> *This morn at after two o'clock, we attacked a party of the rebels, in a place called Dreead in the Co. Kildare, with a party of the Limerick militia, the Canal infantry, Balina and Clonard cavalry. They were soon put to flight, and took to a bog, where many of them fell by the infantry. It is incredible, the way they lived. Horses, cows, sheep &c were found after them, with a number of offensive weapons. They stood to receive but one fire from the infantry when they fled in every direction in the bog which prevented the cavalry*

being of any assistance. They lay under the ditches like pigs, without a tent or any covering. The soldiers from Killcock attacked the rebels at Timahoe (which lay the other side of the bog) at the same time we did. I believe they fled in like manner as with us. I can't tell the number kill'd, but the King's troops burn'd many houses which were deserted by the owners.

    I am Sir
    Your Humble Servt
    Oliver Barker[7]

SOUTH KILDARE

Relatively speaking, there was little action in the south of the county. Despite the mustering of United Irishmen in the area, a three-pronged attack on Athy failed to materialise. The main force of around 600 from Queen's County (Laois) expected the colliers from around the Swan to join them, but they were reluctant, having lost colleagues in an earlier attack on Carlow. The vigorous threats of Colonel Campbell (see Personalities, below), who commanded the military in Athy, added to their fears. These included the installation of a triangle in the town square, an apparatus used to secure victims for public floggings.

The Annals of Ballitore, a personal journal of the poet and diarist Mary Leadbeater (1758–1826), whose grandfather, Abraham Shackleton (1696–1771), taught Edmund Burke (1729–1797) in the village boarding school, recalls the effects of the rebellion on the Quaker community near Athy that shunned violence. They refused military protection and the garrison of Suffolk Fencibles left on 24 May, leaving a rear party of nine men to attend to baggage. The rebels attacked the departing troops and there were casualties on both sides.

Rebels then took over the village. They killed at least one of the rear party and a yeoman lieutenant. They robbed then burned the home of a Reverend Annesley, but did not harm the Quakers. On 26 May Abraham Shackleton successfully arranged a surrender with Colonel Campbell in Athy, but the rebels did not meet the deadline. The following day they heard that Campbell's soldiers were coming to attack them and most of the rebels left Ballitore. The troops arrived and began terrorising the Quakers by brutal searchings and by burning, whipping and killing suspects. Allegedly, in one altercation with straggler rebels, they used a group of Quakers as a human shield. They then went on to attack Timolin, Crookstown and Narraghmore. After the Rebellion, Leadbeater wrote:

> Spring, though remarkably late, clothed the face of nature in more than wonted beauty. Alas, it could not bring to our minds the sensations of gladness which it formerly conveyed. Our hearts dwelt on the recollections that our slaughtered neighbours, our murdered friend and departed child had been enjoying life when last the fields were green.

Throughout the operations, Ballitore villagers attended to both English and Irish casualties.

CASTLEDERMOT

Fifty rebels lost their lives in an abortive attack on Castledermot on 24 May. Their colleagues at Moone dispersed, having been expecting the Castledermot contingent to reinforce their numbers.

MONASTEREVIN AND AREA

Captain Patrick O' Beirne of Nurney led his neighbours and some rebels from Riverstown, Kildoon and Kildangan, about 1,290 in all, against Monasterevin's garrison of cavalry, infantry and yeomen on 24 May. They overran the garrison but an infantry corps under Fredrick Hoystead, augmented by the Bagot family, workers from Cassidy's distillery and from the estate of Lord Tyrawley recaptured the town and held it. These yeomen also joined General Duff at Gibbet Rath (see above).

HAY There!

At Harristown, near Nurney, a priest on the run called to the home of the Hendy family seeking shelter. The farm-owner cut a deep, narrow hole into a rick of hay, put the priest into it and re-shaped the rick. Every day for three weeks, the farmer would go to cut hay and would leave some food for the man in hiding. Soldiers eventually came and searched the Hendy property. They did not find the priest so, when they were gone, the farmer brought the cleric into his house. As he was enjoying its comfort after his uncomfortable ordeal, the soldiers returned to search the one place they had forgotten – the hay-rick! Even in the mid-1950s, Nurney people claimed that the Hendy family prospered due to a blessing left by the priest that 'the Hendys would never want.'

CURSE OF T*he* CASSIDYS

Older natives of Monasterevin alleged that a place known as 'The Weeping Ashes' was the birthplace of Father Edward Prendergast (1749–1798), but people from Rickardstown also claimed him. He received his education in Salamanca where he also studied for the priesthood and was ordained. Upon returning home he became curate at Harristown. During the battle of Monasterevin he visited Barn Hill, where the rebels had camped. Local folklore told how he only went to the area to baptise a sick infant, but whatever his motive, he was captured. On 11 June he was convicted by courtmartial and sentenced to be hanged.

Local tradition claimed that the Cassidys (see above and Industry, Chapter 7) provided the premises for the trial and the rope for the hanging but it did not then own Monasterevin House, the place of trial. It belonged instead to the local yeoman captain, Bagot. The Cassidys had the authority to save one person from the gallows each year, so Father Prendergast sent word to the distillers, seeking a reprieve. They refused, and before he died it was said that he placed a curse on the family, vowing that crows would soon be building nests in the malt-houses and that nobody named Cassidy would be left living in Monasterevin. This was 'The Curse of the Cassidys [on you]', a common Kildare/Carlow malediction. In 1886, however, the poet Gerard Manley Hopkins declared a Miss Cassidy of the brewing family to be 'one of the props and struts of his existence', and the distillery did not close until 1921, after 140 years of business. The Curse of the Cassidy's was tardy in reaching fruition!

Father Prendergast was hanged from a tree beside the River Barrow immediately after his trial. Sir James Duff, of Gibbet Rath infamy, supervised the execution.

The Black Horse Regiment guarded the priest's body that night but, by arrangement, a friendly yeoman supplied them with drink until they became intoxicated. Captain Padraic O'Beirne was a relative of the dead priest and he led a small group of oarsmen up the Barrow from Derryoughta. It was a dark night but folklore claims that a mysterious light directed their course. They seized the corpse and brought it to a place called 'The Diver's Bush', where they placed it in a coffin and bore it to Harristown cemetery.

NARRAGHMORE

Drummers Well is named after a drummer boy of the Suffolk Regiment who beat out a coded message to the insurgents telling them that his unit's ammunition was running out. Tradition claims that his officer decoded the tapping, shot the boy, and dumped his body in the well.

PERSONALITIES OF The REBELLION

SIR FENTON AYLMER, SEVENTH BARONET OF DONADEA (1769–1816)

Son of the Catholic squire, Sir FitzGerald Aylmer (d. 1794) was Sixth Baronet of Donadea Castle, Co. Kildare. His eldest son Sir Fenton Aylmer became High Sheriff of Co. Kildare in 1795. He raised the Donadea Rangers and, along with his namesake, Michael, from nearby Courtown, led this group of three sergeants and thirty troopers. They attempted to track down the rebels in Timahoe, who were led by his kinsman William (below). Some sources deny this, alleging that Sir Fenton was in England during the rebellion.

WILLIAM AYLMER (1778–1820)

From Painestown, Kilcock, William became Colonel of the North Kildare army of the United Irishmen, and gradually imposed discipline on his men. After the battle of Prosperous, he established a camp in an area surrounded by bogland near Timahoe and held out there with up to 3,000 men. When the force eventually surrendered, it was suggested that family friendship with the Marquis of Buckingham averted his execution.

COLONEL BORDEN

The garrison commander at Leixlip beat off early (26 May) rebel attacks on his garrison, on Lucan and on Kilcock, areas for which he was responsible.

COLONEL CAMPBELL

Commander of the Ninth Dragoons in Athy and district commander in south Kildare where he threatened, persecuted and tortured the population. He made flogging official policy. He ordered the arrest of Thomas Reynolds (see below), not knowing that he was a spy. Campbell personally led the party that destroyed Ballitore (see above).

GEORGE CUMMINGS

A Kildare delegate to the Leinster Directory and an apothecary in Kildare town by profession. He was questioned by Captain Swayne (see Prosperous, above) before the rebellion and was arrested during the raid on Oliver Bond's home (see FitzGerald, below).

JOHN JOHNSON DARRAGH

The Co. Kildare gentleman received Secret Service payments and was one of the magistrates attacked in a wave of violence that took place throughout the country early in 1798. He suffered severe wounds.

CAPTAIN JOHN DOORLEY (C. 1771–1798)

This Lullymore insurgent was active in Rathangan, Ovidstown and other areas throughout the rebellion. He deserted from Spencer's yeomanry, was captured and was probably hanged in Mullingar, Co. Westmeath.

MICHAEL DOORLEY (1772–1808)

Brother of John, from Lullymore, Co. Kildare, Doorley was involved in a number of acts of aggression (see Rathangan, above). He wore uniform, liked to be addressed as 'Colonel' and manufactured bullets from lead, pewter dishes and cutlery. He led a company of men from Lullymore, Allen and Rathangan and was strongly associated with the murder of Spencer.[8]

GENERAL SIR RALPH DUNDAS

The elderly, almost blind District Commander of the midlands had his headquarters at Castlemartin, Kilcullen. Although reasonably humane, he adopted a disciplinary attitude in seeking surrender of weapons that gave his subordinates excuses for using harsh methods in carrying out searches. These led to the early rebel attacks on garrisons in the north of the county—Prosperous, Naas and Clane. Dundas later defeated the rebels at the Bridge of Kilcullen, but then retreated to Naas and ordered other garrisons to do likewise. Only Athy did not comply—rebels killed the messenger bearing the retreat order. This inept action meant that the rebels held most of Co. Kildare, thus virtually blockading Dublin. He parleyed with the rebels at Knockaulin Hill and succeeded in persuading them to abandon their camp and leave their weapons piled high on the hill. Lord Camden disapproved of the lenient terms Dundas had offered but another truce situation was already in motion (see Gibbet Rath above). To the authorities, Dundas became a figure of fun and rebels regarded him as a man without honour.

CAPTAIN ERSKINE (D. 1798)

Erskine led arms searches against the Co. Kildare rebels. With Cornet Love he was particularly destructive in Ballitore. He led the Ninth Dragoons at Kilcullen (see Dundas, above).

DOCTOR JOHN ESMONDE (1760–1798)

This United Irishman from Osberstown was a brother of Sir John Esmonde, a Catholic baronet from Wexford. A reserved member of the Kildare executive of the United Irishmen, he is believed to have planned the attack on Prosperous and Naas. He was captured and hanged from Carlisle Bridge, Dublin, with his coat turned inside out–the sign of a deserter.

LORD EDWARD FITZGERALD (1763–1798)

Son of James Edward (1722–1773) First Duke of Leinster (see introduction to Chapter 7) and Emilia Mary Lennox, daughter of the Duke of Richmond. He was great-great grandson of Charles II (1630–1685). Edward FitzGerald was born in London but lived from an early age at Carton, Maynooth. He became his emotional mother's favourite because as a child he threatened to hit her with a poker. This, she believed, showed spirit. She took her family to France to avoid the social opprobrium that went with marrying their tutor after James Henry's death. She bought Edward a commission in the British army and he was slightly wounded at Eutaw Springs (1781) during the American War of Independence (1775–83). Back in Ireland he represented Athy (1783) in Parliament before resuming military life in Canada. Yet again, he returned to Ireland and became MP for Co. Kildare (1790). He was opposed to autocratic rule and Tom Paine's writing influenced his politics, focussing his idealism on republicanism.

While living in London in 1790, FitzGerald had an affair with the estranged wife of playwright Richard Brinsley Sheridan (1751–1816). She was the 'Maid of Bath' (d. 1792), an accomplished singer forbidden to continue her career by Sheridan after their marriage. She had a daughter by FitzGerald but died of consumption shortly after giving birth.

Edward followed Paine to Paris to become 'Le Citoyen Edouard FitzGerald'. While there, he fell in love with Pamela, daughter of Madame de Genlis, probably from a liaison with the former Duc d'Orléans. In appearance, Pamela bore a striking resemblance to Sheridan's wife. About this time, FitzGerald lost his commission as a result of toasting the abolition of hereditary titles at a gathering of British residents.

After a passionate courtship and a December 1792 marriage in Paris, he and Pamela later returned to Blackrock, Co. Dublin. A rumour of the time stated that she wore a red neckerchief, claiming that it was dyed in the blood of Louis XVI (1754–1793), the deposed King of France, who had been tried for treason and guillotined in 1793 (denouncing her royalist connections in deference to the man she loved, perhaps!).

The couple and their child moved to live alongside Kildare Castle, on the east side of the market square in Kildare town, in a house called Leinster Lodge. FitzGerald once wrote to his mother about the place. The note suggests that he was a keen gardener:

> My little place is much improved by the few things I have done and by my planting. By the bye, I doubt if I told you of my flower garden; I got a great deal from Frescati. I have been in Kildare since Pam's lying-in and it looks delightful, though all the leaves were off the trees, but so comfortable and snug. I think I shall pass a delightful winter there. I have got two fine clumps [clamps?] of turf which look so comfortable and pretty. I have paled my little flower garden before my hall door with a lath paling like the cottage and stuck it full of roses, sweet briar, honeysuckle and Spanish broom. I have got all my beds ready for my flowers so you may guess how I long to be down to plant them.
>
> The little fellow will be a great addition to the party. I think when I am down there with Pam and child, of a blustering evening, with a good turf fire and a pleasant book, coming in after seeing my poultry up, my garden settled, flower-beds and plants covered for fear of frost; the place looking comfortable and taken care of, I shall be as happy as possible; and since I am, I shall regret nothing but not being near my dearest mother, and her not being one of our party. It is indeed a drawback and a great one, our not being more together. Dear Malvern, how pleasant we were then: you can't think how this time of year puts me in mind of it.
>
> Your affectionate son,
> E.F.[9]

When Lord Edward FitzGerald was returning to his Kildare home from the Curragh one day in 1795, officers of the Dragoons Regiment stationed at the military camp upbraided him for wearing a green cravat. They demanded its removal, FitzGerald refused and a colleague suggested a duel, which the officers declined, withdrawing to their quarters. At the next military ball in the camp no woman would accept a dance from the cowardly gentlemen.

FitzGerald joined the United Irishmen and went to France with Arthur O'Connor to organise French assistance for a revolution. Aware of his wife's ancestry, the French Directory were wary of negotiating, so FitzGerald returned and headed a military committee of the United

Irishmen. He denounced martial law and prepared for rebellion with or without French assistance.

On 12 March 1798 he escaped a raid on the Leinster Directory of the United Irishmen. It was meeting in the Lower Bridge Street home of Oliver Bond (1760–1798), a Dublin woollen merchant and a leader of the movement. Lord Edward went on the run. Major Henry Charles Sirr (1764–1841), the Town Major, harassed the United Irishmen and seized FitzGerald at his Thomas Street hide-out on 19 May 1798. Lord Edward killed a member of the raiding party but received wounds and died on 4 June 1798 in Newgate Prison.

LADY PAMELA FITZGERALD

Lord Edward's arrest brought on his wife Pamela's early confinement. She was expelled on a charge of complicity with her late husband and went to Hamburg. She later remarried.

RICHARD GRIFFITH (C. 1752–1820)

The Dublin-born captain of the Clane Yeomanry was a director of the Grand Canal Company (see Canals, Chapter 7). He lived in Millicent. He was Askeaton, Co. Limerick MP (1783–90) and High Sheriff of Co. Kildare (1788). At a May meeting in Naas in 1797 he was among a group that called on the Lord Lieutenant to proclaim Co. Kildare. That amounted almost to imposition of martial law and what today's society would call 'zero tolerance'.

RICHARD GRIFFITH (1784–1878)

Son of the above, Dublin-born Sir Richard John Griffith lived in Portarlington, Co. Laois and in Millicent. Later, he became a mining engineer and geologist famous for Griffith's Valuation of Rateable Property in Ireland (1848–64). He was a pupil in Rathangan during the rebellion and when rebels attacked his school he thought it wise to adopt their custom of wearing a green sprig in his hat. The rebels left, but a group of dragoons attacked the school and executed its head-master. Only the intervention of a local magistrate saved Griffith. He joined the Royal Artillery in 1799 but resigned his commission to study engineering.

HEPENSTALL

See 'Walking Gallows', below.

FATHER MOGUE KEARNS

Father Kearns was one of the chief leaders of the rebels in Wexford. Having marched a force of rebels from Three Rocks to Newtownbarry (Bunclody) he took the town, but a counter-attack by its garrison inflicted heavy casualties on his force and dispersed it. In disarray, he and his army of 4,000 arrived at Timahoe to join Aylmer, who was short of provisions. Considering his welcome less than warm, he marched through Co. Meath where he attacked Clonard. He then moved on to Co. Louth but, receiving no encouragement, he returned to Co. Kildare.

There is a place known as the Wheel About, near Rathangan. Its name comes from an incident that took place in 1798. At Clonbullogue, Co. Offaly, people informed Father Mogue Kearns that there were Redcoats in the area. He asked a smith to take off his horse's shoes and re-nail them backwards. He thought the enemy would think a rider had gone the opposite direction. The ruse failed and he was captured near Rathangan and made to 'wheel about' to Edenderry, where he was hanged.

GEORGE LUBE (SOMETIMES LOOBY OR LUBEY. D.C. 1803)

From Corcoranstown, Colonel Lube was a prominent Kildare leader, operating alongside William Aylmer, above. After the rebellion he was imprisoned in Kilmainham gaol until 1802. When refused a number of petitions he was transported to an undisclosed destination. Some reports say that it was America while others suggest that he escaped custody, made his way to America and died there shortly after arrival.

ROGER MCGARRY

When General Wilford abandoned Kildare, this leader of the Kildare United Irishmen occupied the town.

BELLA MARTIN

A Belfast woman who worked in Painestown House, home of William Aylmer. She informed on the rebels. The authorities may have arranged her employment at Painestown for that purpose.

EDWARD MOLLOY (D. 1798)

From Mount Prospect, Rathangan, Molloy was a yeoman turned insurgent who fought at Rathangan. Subsequently, he was hanged from a gate pier (or a lamppost, according to a ballad in his memory).

CAPTAIN MICHAEL QUIGLEY

One of William Aylmer's officers in North Kildare, Quigley made a sortie from Timahoe and ambushed a force near Clongowes Wood. In 1804 he was arrested for his participation in Robert Emmet's (1778–1803) abortive 1803 rebellion.

MICHAEL REYNOLDS (D. 1798)

A member of the Kildare Committee, and National Directory member, Michael's calls for the assassination of his namesake, Thomas, (see below) went unheeded. A farmer from Johnstown, he was a driving force behind the rising in Kildare. He led the attack on Naas and fled to Wicklow after losing the battle and his horse. On 25 June he received wounds at the Battle of Hacketstown, Co. Carlow, and died some days later.

THOMAS REYNOLDS (1771–1836)

The most despised informer of the rebellion was Thomas Reynolds, married to Harriet Witherington, sister of Wolfe Tone's wife. The son of a Dublin textile merchant, he was educated in Liège. After inheriting his father's considerable business, he was swindled by an associate of the firm and became bankrupt. He joined the United Irishmen and reached the rank of colonel, organising in south Kildare. He became frightened when he learned of the plans for a rebellion. Through an intermediary named Cope, the Under Secretary, Edward Cooke, was offering large sums of money for information. Reynolds informed Dublin Castle of the meeting of the Leinster Directory of the United Irishmen on 12 March at the home of Oliver Bond. For this, he received a lump sum of £5,000, an annual pension of £1,000 and employment with the British service abroad.

HAMILTON ROWAN (1751–1834)

Born in London, the son of a wealthy landowner, Archibald Hamilton Rowan was a distinguished United Irishman. He was educated at Westminster and Queen's College, Cambridge. Around 1770, he served as a Lieutenant Colonel in the Portuguese army. He married in Paris and returned to Ireland in 1784 to settle, first at Two-Mile-House, then in Rathcoffey. He was a founder member of the Northern Whig Club, Belfast. A member of the Volunteers, he joined the United Irishmen in 1792. He and the prominent United Irishman, Napper Tandy (1740–1803), attended a Volunteer meeting in Dublin wearing uniform and side arms. He distributed an address calling 'Citizen Soldiers to Arms' and was arrested in January 1793 and tried a year later. He was fined £500 and imprisoned but escaped and fled to France in a small craft. In 1795 he went to the United States and met Wolfe Tone and Napper Tandy. He was a strong supporter of Catholic Emancipation but atrocities seen in France during its revolution left him reluctant to return to Ireland during the rebellion. He received permission to return to England in 1806 and came back to Ireland that same year.

JAMES SPENCER

An elderly agent of the Duke of Leinster, he surrendered to rampaging rebels in Rathangan but they butchered him and displayed his corpse on his front door.

CAPTAIN RICHARD LONGFORD SWAYNE (D. 1798)

Commander of the Royal Cork City Regiment of Militia in Prosperous, Co. Kildare (see Prosperous, above).

THEOBALD WOLFE TONE (1763–1798)

Biographical details of Wolfe Tone provide a background to the rebellion itself. A Protestant coachman's son, the most celebrated of the United

Irishmen was born in Stafford Street, Dublin. He was educated in Trinity College and at London's Middle Temple. He married sixteen-year-old Matilda Witherington and they lived for a while at his father's home in Blackhall, Clane, and in nearby Bodenstown. A qualified lawyer, he preferred politics to the bar. In 1791, he published a pamphlet outlining the injustices suffered by Irish Roman Catholics. Enthusiastic about France's revolution, he joined Napper Tandy and Thomas Russell (1767–1803) in founding the United Irishmen. His ideology, still quoted by republican activists, if not always abided by, was aimed at breaking the connection with England, 'the never failing source of all our political evils [and substituting] the common name of Irishman in place of the denominations of Protestant, Catholic and dissenter'. Dissatisfied with the contents of the 1793 Catholic Relief Act, he looked to France for help. The authorities became aware of this and ordered him to leave the country. He and his family left Ireland, sailing from Belfast in May 1795.

In Philadelphia he received an entrée to France, travelled there and persuaded its new ruling Directory to accept him into the army and to invade Ireland, joining with its revolutionaries to end British rule. In 1796, Tone and Hoche (1768–1797) attempted to land at Bantry but failed. Later, Tone attempted to raise a Dutch force but was unsuccessful. Further attempts to initiate another major French expedition failed—only Humbert's ill-prepared landing at Killala in August 1798 made any impression.

In September 1798, under General Bombard and with 3,000 men, he eventually sailed again but was arrested in Lough Swilly on 12 October. At his courtmartial in Dublin on 10 November, he appeared dressed in his French uniform. He was sentenced to death by hanging but committed suicide on the morning fixed for his execution. Using a knife, he slashed his windpipe instead of his jugular vein, and is alleged to have said to his doctor, 'I find I am but a bad anatomist.' He died on 19 November.

A ballad of Tone by Alice Milligan (1866–1953) includes the lines:

> *The first storm of winter blew high, blew high;*
> *Red leaves were scattering to a gloomy sky;*
> *Rain clouds were lowering o'er the plains of Kildare,*
> *When from Dublin, southward, the mourners came there.*

> *'In the spring,' they whispered, 'Lord Edward bled.*
> *And the blood of hosts was in summer shed;*
> *Death in the autumn o'er Connacht passed,*
> *But the loss that is sorest came last, came last.*

It is considered almost obligatory for people of all shades of republicanism to affirm their cause at the grave of Wolfe Tone, in Bodenstown, near Sallins. Maeve Cavanagh McDowell's ballad is also well known. Part of it goes:

> *The lush grass hides forgotten graves,*
> *The elders are abloom*
> *An ivied wall stands sentinel*
> *Beside a lonely tomb.*
> *And here, while summer holds her sway,*
> *Linnet and blackbird throng,*
> *And blend their sweetest songs o'er him*
> *Who loved the battle song.*

Thomas Davis's (1814–1845) poem, too:

> *In Bodenstown churchyard there is a green grave,*
> *And wildly around it the winter winds rave;*
> *Small shelter I ween are the ruined walls there*
> *When the storm sweeps down o'er the plains of Kildare . . .*

'WALKING GALLOWS'

A greatly hated Wicklow man, Lieutenant Edward Hepenstall (d. 1800), received the nickname 'Walking Gallows' because he hanged rebels by throwing the hangman's noose around their necks and tugging it over his shoulder as his giant frame strode along roads. Even before the rebellion, he admitted to his *modus operandi* when giving testimony at Athy court in September 1797. There is evidence of at least one hanging by him in Carbury. He encountered a suspicious looking man there, and without any evidence, decided he had to be a rebel plotting the death of the king and so disposed of him.

HUGH WARE (1772–1846)

Initially a planner of the rebellion with Lord Edward FitzGerald, Ware was under close observation by the authorities and tried to leave the country. Unsuccessful, he joined William Aylmer (see above) and became his second-in-command at Timahoe. He encouraged the eventual surrender in Co. Kildare and negotiated terms. Imprisoned in Kilmainham Jail, he studied military strategy and tactics. Influential family connections secured his release in April 1802 after which he went to France. He hoped to revive the rebellion with French aid, joined the Irish Regiment and had a distinguished career (see Firmount House, Chapter 9).

GENERAL WILFORD

Commander of Kildare garrison, Richard Wilford obeyed Dundas (above) and vacated the town. He foolishly left a stockpile of seized arms and pikes behind which the rebels duly retrieved.

THOMAS WOGAN BROWNE (1758–1812)

From Castlebrowne (Clongowes Wood), Wogan Browne supported Catholic Emancipation. A Liberal, he met frequently with Tone, Russell, and Rowan but remained loyal to the Crown. He committed suicide in 1812.

CANALS To COUNTRY CLUBS

7

The 1800 ACT OF UNION created the United Kingdom of Great Britain and Ireland. It provided for four bishops and twenty-eight representative peers in the House of Lords and 100 Members of Parliament (MPs) at the House of Commons. Two Co. Kildare Members were elected in 1801. They were Maurice Keating and John La Touche (one source names him Peter in the 1802 election). Robert La Touche represented the county from 1802 until 1826. Lord R.S. FitzGerald partnered him from 1802 to 1813. FitzGerald resigned then and Lord W.C. O'Brien FitzGerald won a by-election and served until 1831. The names of many of the other MPs for the county have survived and can be found in Appendix 1.

Augustus Fredrick FitzGerald (1791–1874), Third Duke of Leinster, supported Catholic Emancipation and parliamentary reform and was Grand Master of the Freemasons of Ireland. The Whig, Edward George G. Stanley (1799–1869), Fourteenth Earl Derby and Lord Lieutenant, wrote him the 'Stanley Letter'. It was the basis for an undenominational national education system 'from which would be banished forever the suspicion of proselytism and which, admitting children of all religious persuasions, should not interfere with the peculiar tenets of any'.

FitzGerald was Chairman of the Board of Commissioners for National Education, established in 1831, that included Protestant and Catholic

Archbishops of Dublin. He was active in a number of social and policing initiatives in Co. Kildare. These included a county infirmary, a police barracks at Donadea and a school for Kildare town. He spoke on Catholic Emancipation, reform of the representative peerage systems, distress in Prosperous, the Peace Preservation Act of 1821 and the admission of Catholics to the Dublin Guild of Merchants. He attacked the Kildare Place Society saying that, while it promoted education of the poor, it indulged in compulsory bible reading and proselytism. He disagreed with Daniel O'Connell's (1775–1847) efforts to repeal the 1800 Act of Union and convened an anti-Repeal meeting in 1830. (O'Connell's campaign flourished and in 1843 he spoke at one of his most successful 'monster rallies', at Mullamast, where an estimated 4,000 people attended.)

After FitzGerald's appointment as Lieutenant of Co. Kildare in 1831 he was active in the county's elections of 1832, 1835 and 1837 and in tithe agitation. He championed the retention of Athy as the county's second assize town, and he backed the payment of an increased grant to Maynooth College (see below) to which he was appointed as a Visitor. A June 1845 Act of Parliament increased the state's grant to the college from £8,928 to £26,350 and allotted a building fund.

In mid-century he espoused several causes affecting the county: the Dublin-Mullingar turnpike road, a bill for the better regulation of medical charities, elections of 1854, 1859 and 1874, Kildare Militia's establishment as a rifle corps, the application of the Towns Improvement Act to Athy, the proclamation of South Kildare under the Peace Preservation Act 1866, a visit from the Prince of Wales to Carton (1868) and the initiation of the Church Representative Body.

CANALS

Meanwhile, the stated object of a 1715 Act of Parliament was 'to Encourage the Draining and Improving of the Bogs and Unprofitable Low Grounds and for Easing and Despatching the Inland Carriage and Conveyance of Goods from One Part to Another Within this Kingdom.' In pursuit of this goal the rivers Liffey, Rye and Boyne feature, but an attempt to make the Liffey navigable during the 1720s was a costly failure.

THE GRAND CANAL

A statute of 1751 allowed the Irish parliament to establish a body of Commissioners of Inland Navigation. Its most ambitious project was the Grand Canal's 267 kilometres of waterway which served a number of towns before it reached the River Barrow in 1791, and the River Shannon in 1805. Eighteen kilometres from its Dublin terminus the canal enters Co. Kildare, near Hazelhatch, Celbridge.

The Dublin-Barrow construction began in 1756 and traffic was floating from Dublin to Sallins by 1779. There was consternation when the route being excavated began swinging westward after Sallins. Wealthy businessmen who staunchly supported Dublin Castle dominated the Grand Canal Company. Co. Kildare people called them 'Castle Hacks'. Unwilling to be overlooked, landlords and merchants in the Naas area formed the Co. of Kildare Canal Company and began constructing a 3.2 kilometre branch from Soldiers' Island, Sallins in 1786. The company went bankrupt but the Grand Canal Company then took over. Not only did it complete the Naas branch, but it continued on to Corbally Harbour, near Athgarvan, presumably to serve a local (Reeves') mill and perhaps the Curragh Camp.

The branch, the most elevated on the canal, cost £30,000 and needed five locks and three bridges. Two attempts at establishing a passenger service failed but it gradually built up a significant cargo trade.

Over 3 kilometres south of the Soldiers' Island junction, the canal crosses the Liffey at the impressive 160 metre, seven-arched Leinster aqueduct. The Blackwood feeder, taking waters from a reservoir at Ballynafagh, joins the canal before its one mile straight into Robertstown.

The passenger hotel in Robertstown is late eighteenth century (it opened for business in 1801) and the canal village has its original bridge and quayside installations. Beyond the village, at Lowtown, the Barrow branch supplied by the Milltown feeder heads off through Rathangan and Monasterevin, towns to which the canal brought considerable benefits in its heyday. During the Great Famine, bandits carried out raids on traffic along this stretch. A landlord, John Dopping, anticipated this when he wrote to the Under-Secretary in 1846 remarking on the existence of distress in the 'populous district' thereabouts. Over twenty constables were assigned to protecting the provision boats. Despite their attention, the City of Dublin Steam Packet Company was forced to inform the Under Secretary that a mob stole 'several packages of tobacco, eggs and whiskey' in December 1847. The poor souls were hoping to have some semblance of a happy Christmas, perhaps!

After Monasterevin, the branch leaves Co. Kildare and takes a course parallel to the Barrow before re-visiting the county to join the river at Athy. The main canal continues on through Allenwood and Ticknevin and finally leaves Co. Kildare just short of an aqueduct south of Edenderry. The canal's hey-day was between 1870 and 1880 when it carried almost 380,000 tonnes of cargo. Commodities included coal, manure, porter, limestone, flour, turf (peat), bricks, grain and other sundries.

The quickening pace of industry gradually made canal haulage uneconomical and the last barge-load of Guinness passed through Kildare on its way to Limerick on 27 May 1960. Córas Iompair Éireann (CIÉ) closed the canal in 1961 and it became derelict.

Plans to fill in the Naas branch aroused local opposition and restoration began. New lock gates were installed, and in 1987 a boat rally took place. By 1989 all was complete and the old harbour stores became a youth centre. In 1978 the Grand and Royal Canals (see below) and the Barrow navigation were transferred from CIE to the Office of Public Works and gradual improvements began to take place. Cruiser and barge tourism developed and canal tow paths provided walks and stands for coarse fishermen.

The ROYAL CANAL

Despite the company's name, John Binns, a Dublin silk wholesaler who spearheaded the Royal Canal Company, held radical political views. An opponent of the establishment, his Liberal colleagues called him 'Long John Binns' while his opponents referred to him as 'The Devil's Darning Needle'. The 145 kilometre waterway from Dublin to Tarmonbarry on the Shannon in Co. Longford had been mooted long before the Charter of the Royal Canal Company was enrolled in 1789. William Robert FitzGerald, the Second Duke of Leinster (1780–1803), a Whig, was among its promoters. He was accused of prevailing on planners to bring the canal line south of a more desirable northern route through Co. Meath in order to serve 'his' town of Maynooth.

Construction began in 1790. Workers were paid ten pence per day. They resented this being less than Grand Canal rates and protested until their employers rectified the situation. Slow progress and mounting costs became the subject of an inquiry. Instead of an estimated £7,500, the Rye Water embankment near Leixlip cost £28,231. The inquiry report carried a veiled criticism of the route taken to accommodate Maynooth:

> Whether the Canal from the Broadstone up to Kilcock and thro' the Bog of Cappa [gh] was in the first instance fairly and impartially laid out for the public benefit or the advantage of the Canal Company, or whether the money was well expended is no part of [the inquiry].[1]

The canal was never a great success. It brought vegetables and turf to Dublin and, ironically, returned with coal! In the 1820s, armed Ribbonmen, local members of the agrarian Ribbon Societies, similar to the eighteenth century Whiteboys, attacked barges and campaigned for higher wages for horse drivers. If the company dismissed a driver, the Ribbonmen threatened his replacement, so that:

> [The drivers who] were correct and attentive were unmercifully beat and turned off the canal, and those that [remained did] as they please[d].[2]

Soldiers from the 40th Regiment of Foot stationed in Naas frequently guarded embankments against deliberate breaching that was aimed at creating employment for repairmen. There were reports of the Ribbonmen being drunk, firing guns indiscriminately and 'using irritating expressions on religious subjects, which is by no means proper in the present state of the country'.

The Royal Canal enters Co. Kildare near Confey Abbey, Leixlip, passes through Maynooth and leaves the county shortly after Kilcock–a brief incursion.

DUELLING AND FIGHTING

In 1813, Naas received a new military barracks and in 1815 the town was the probable location of a duel. It arose out of Daniel O'Connell's campaign for Catholic rights, during which he referred to the champion of Orangemen, Chief Secretary Robert Peel (1788–1850) as 'Orange Peel'. That was in 1812, two years before O'Connell berated Dublin Corporation for neglect of Catholics.

A member called D'Esterre took issue. He represented the Guild of Merchants and was seeking the appointment of High Sheriff. After some correspondence, threats to horse-whip 'The Liberator' and verbal baiting, a duel between the pair took place on 2 February 1815. Some sources claim that it took place at Lyons House, Celbridge but most agree that it was at Bishopscourt, near Naas (see Fine Houses, below). O'Connell shot his opponent in the bladder. Surgeon Peile, Deputy Inspector to the Forces of Law and Order, was there in disguise and attended to D'Esterre but he died the next day after making a statement holding O'Connell blameless.

A fight of another kind involved Dan Donnelly (d. 1820), who fought an English pugilist named Hall for a purse of 100 guineas in 1814. Over 40,000 witnessed his victory at the Curragh. A great victory parade headed for Dublin with Donnelly's mother sitting in an open landau pulled by four white horses. The entourage stopped at every public house and reached Dublin seventeen days later. Mrs Donnelly stood to acknowledge the applause of the crowd, slapped her ample bosom and boasted 'these are the breasts that fed the champion'. Donnelly allegedly spent his winnings in two weeks. The following year, he defeated the English champion, George Cooper, at 'Donnelly's Hollow' and people still walk in his 'footsteps' there.

> Ten to one on Cooper, before he struck a blow
> But he little knew that in Donnelly he had met his overthrow.

Donnelly's long arm was on display in a Kilcullen public house for many years.

DEVELOPMENTS ON TRACK

In 1816, the remains of the historic priory of Great Connell were demolished and the stone was used to build Newbridge Cavalry Barracks. Also in that year the potato crop failed, causing famine and a typhus epidemic that lasted until 1819. A fever epidemic in 1826 adversely affected the textile industry in Co. Kildare. Daniel O' Connell was elected MP for Co. Clare in 1828 and aroused passions countrywide. Fearing another rebellion, Robert Peel, the then Prime Minister, conceded on Catholic Emancipation and the Catholic Relief Act became law in 1829.

In January 1845 the Duke of Leinster came from Carton to Adamstown, near Lucan. There he dug the first sod for a railway line from Dublin to Kildare. A cynical Kildareman present shouted 'I can die happy after seeing a Duke working like any common man'. Within six months the celebrated railway engineer William Dargan had brought the line from Hazelhatch, Celbridge, to Sallins. The Duke of Leinster, Sir Gerald George Aylmer of Donadea, Robert Mackey Wilson of Coolcarrigan House and other prominent landowners proposed a branch line to Edenderry from Maynooth, via Killadoon, Staplestown, Timahoe and Carbury. Christopher Rynd of Mountarmstrong objected to the route and caused the collapse of the proposition.

Further progress into Kildare was rapid and traffic opened in 1846. The first stage included a branch to Carlow from Cherryville, near Kildare town. This now serves Athy, Carlow, Kilkenny and Waterford.

Monasterevin is the meeting place of canal, railway, highway and the noble River Barrow. The long viaduct that bears the Cork railway line is known as 'Hellfire Jack's Bridge'. After its opening, allegedly, the driver of the first steam train across shouted, 'Now, for hell or Cork'.

At 3 a.m. on 31 March 1976, Ireland's 'Great Train Robbery' took place near Sallins. An armed gang placed detonators on the line. Normally, these are warning signals and when one raider waved a red light on the track, the engine driver stopped the train. The man with the light forced the driver to reverse to a spot where colleagues and transport were waiting. Meanwhile, in the mail car, post office officials had completed their sorting. Sacks of registered mail with cash for Dublin banks carried red labels and in just fifteen minutes the raiders removed twelve bags, containing about £221,000.

A serious accident occurred near Cherryville Junction on 21 August 1983. The Dublin-bound evening service from Tralee failed and a following train from Galway crashed into it. Eight people were killed and thirty injured, but the disaster might have been far worse since up to 500 passengers, mostly children, were aboard the trains.

In March 1847 a test run was made on a line from Dublin to Enfield by placing seats in horse-drawn goods wagons as no locomotive was yet available. From 28 June, however, Leixlip, Maynooth, Kilcock and Enfield enjoyed a full service with four each-way trips daily.

Train travel fell into the doldrums after World War Two but picked up again when cars began clogging roads into the cities. By the twenty-first century, the Dublin-Cork and Dublin-Sligo lines were serving thousands of Co. Kildare commuters.

EDUCATION AND T*he* 'BIG HOUSES'

The many castles, such as those at Kilkea, Maynooth, Athy and Kilteel, the ruined religious houses at Kildare and the Franciscan abbeys at Clane, Castledermot and Celbridge link the medieval world with the modern. Fine medieval houses included Jigginstown House, Naas (c. 1636) where the Lord Deputy, Thomas Wentworth, Earl of Strafford hoped to entertain King Charles I (1625–1649). A Dutchman, John Allen, is credited with its design. It was one of the earliest brick buildings in Ireland and would have been the largest had its design been fully implemented. The tradition continued and grand mansions emerged, often through reconstruction of earlier structures, in the eighteenth and nineteenth centuries. Some became renowned places of learning, more fell into decay and a few survived to serve new purposes.

MAYNOOTH COLLEGE

The FitzGeralds already had a long association with Maynooth College, one of two distinctive Irish educational establishments in Co. Kildare. During the era of Penal Laws, Irish youths aspiring to the Roman Catholic priesthood had received their education and ordination on the continent, mainly in France. The French Revolution (1789–99) resulted in the closing of many of its colleges. This, and the danger of young clerics returning with revolutionary views, resulted in the government responding to pressure from the Irish Hierarchy by endowing the foundation of Maynooth College in an Act of Parliament (1795). The site was on lands acquired from the Duke of Leinster, beside his castle.

At the end of the first half-century of its existence, half of Ireland's clergy had received their training in Maynooth. Students who arrived on horseback often sold their mounts at the Friday market held on the green outside the college. The lay college operated until 1817 and its theological college became a pontifical university in 1896. The National University has recognised the college's university status since 1913.

Reverend Nicholas Callan (1799–1864), Professor of Natural Philosophy at the college from 1826 to 1864, pioneered electrical science and invented the induction coil. The college museum holds some of his apparatus.

An early distinguished visitor to the college was in pursuit of a stag. She was Elizabeth, (1837–1898) Empress of Austria and Queen of Hungary, and the year was 1879. She received a warm welcome and returned later to attend Mass. King Edward VII (1841–1910) visited the college on his third visit to Ireland in 1907, an event that was almost overlooked because of the disappearance of the 'crown jewels' (regalia of the Knights of Saint Patrick) from Dublin Castle. The college president, Doctor Daniel Mannix (1864–1963), was a nationalist and resented flying the Union Flag. Instead, he raised the king's racing colours. The Catholic Church's interest in his enthusiasm for horses amused His Majesty!

Other distinguished foreign guests visiting Maynooth College included Prince Rainier (1923–) and Princess Grace (1929–1982) of Monaco with their children Caroline and Albert, in 1963; Pope John Paul II (1920–) in 1979; His Excellency Francesco Cossiga, President of Italy (1928–) and King Juan Carlos I of Spain (1938–), both in 1986.

CLONGOWES WOOD COLLEGE

Other prominent Co. Kildare family names are associated with its second educational establishment, Clongowes Wood College. Early occupants of Clongowes Castle (c. 1558–1636) a border fort of the Pale near Clane, included the FitzEustace family. A Dublin merchant, Thomas Browne purchased the property from Richard Reynell in 1667 and descendants of that family, extended the castle between 1718 and 1788 and changed its name from Clongowes Castle to Castle Browne. Like many Irish castles, Clongowes had its lore. When a Browne was killed in battle in Austria, his ghost appeared to his sister back home. On another occasion, Archibald Hamilton Rowan (see Chapter 6) from Rathcoffey was sheltering in Clongowes Wood when soldiers arrived to arrest him. They tried to force an entry and bullet holes from their weapons remained in the door of the castle for centuries. Horseshoe prints leading to the stables behind convinced them that Hamilton Rowan was there but he had escaped on a horse that Browne had shod backwards to delude his friend's pursuers (a ruse that appears regularly in folk accounts–see Father Mogue Kearns, Personalities, Chapter 6).

Bronze-Age implements discovered near Bishopsland (*National Museum of Ireland*)

Ink and pencil drawing of St Brigid by Reverend Jack Hanlon (*National Gallery of Ireland*)

(*Above*) East face of
Moone High Cross
(*Dúchas The Heritage
Service*)

(*Left*) The Twelve
Apostles, from
Moone High Cross
(*East Coast and
Midlands Regional
Tourism Authority*)

The 32.3 metre Round Tower at Kildare (*Dúchas The Heritage Service*)

(*Above*) Maynooth Castle
(*Dúchas The Heritage Service*)

(*Left*) Garret Óg FitzGerald,
Ninth Earl of Kildare

(*Above*) Castletown House, Celbridge (*Bord Fáilte*)

(*Left*) Theobald Wolfe Tone (*Ulster Museum*)

Lord Edward FitzGerald by Hugh Douglas Hamilton (*National Gallery of Ireland*)

(*Above*) Carton House,
engraving from c. 1826

(*Left*) The Grand Salon in
Carton House, Maynooth
(*Bord Fáilte*)

(*Above*) Bishopscourt,
Naas, from an old
engraving

(*Left*) Right Honourable
William Conolly
(*National Gallery of Ireland*)

Early County Kildare cottiers (*Culver Pictures*)

(*Above*) Maynooth College
c. 1900 (*National Library of
Ireland, Lawrence Collection*)

(*Left*) Robertstown, showing
canal and original Grand
Canal Hotel (*Bord Fáilte*)

Colonel Patrick Brennan, Assistant Commissioner (in car) in Kildare Barracks
during the 'Kildare Mutiny' of 1922
(*Presented to Seán Spellissy by the late Michael Lehane, Cregg*)

The Cyclist Company, 4 Battalion, parading at Sallins on 23 June 1918
(*Bureau of Military History 1913–21 Collection*)

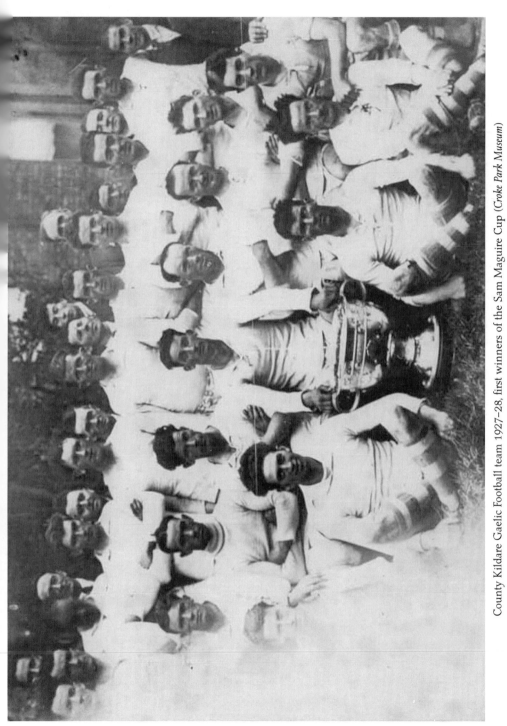

County Kildare Gaelic Football team 1927–28, first winners of the Sam Maguire Cup (*Croke Park Museum*)

Milling peat, 1961 (*Morrison*, The Emergent Years, *1984*)

Athy town, from
the air (*Cambridge
University Collection*)

Kilkea Castle today
(*East Coast and Midlands Regional Tourism Authority*)

The only example of a mid-eighteenth-century Arcadian garden in Europe: Larchill, Kilcock (*KELT*)

Racing at 'Peerless Punchestown' (*KELT*)

'The plains of Kildare': An aerial view in the Athy–Castledermot area (*Cambridge University Collection*)

In 1813, before leaving to fight with Napoleon I (1769–1821), General Michael Wogan Browne, ADC to the King of Saxony, sold the castle to the Society of Jesus (Jesuits) who restored the name Clongowes Wood. Pope Clement XIV (d. 1774) had suppressed the order in 1773, but after its rehabilitation by Pope Pius VII (d. 1823) in 1814, Father Peter Kenney (1779–1841) established the Collegium Maximum for Ireland at Clongowes Wood. Allegedly, Edmund Ignatius Rice (1762–1844), founder of the Irish Christian Brothers assisted him in return for support and advice in his own educational endeavours. A south Dublin site was available and would have been more suitable but for anti-Roman Catholic and anti-Jesuit prejudices prevailing in and around the city at the time. The education of scholars began in May 1814 and within four years 250 pupils were enrolled. This called for urgent action, especially when fever broke out, probably due to overcrowding. The building of extensions began immediately. The fine lime trees lining the main drive to the college once extended to Betaghstown, a mile distant.

BARBERSTOWN CASTLE

Originally thirteenth century, the tower house that now forms part of a hotel has eighteenth and nineteenth century additions. It had associations with de Penkinstons, Suttons and Bartons (see Straffan, Chapter 9). Tradition tells how its lease once stipulated expiry when the tenant 'was put underground'. After his death, clever family members interred him in the wall of the castle, so leaving him over ground and the lease secure.

BISHOPSCOURT HOUSE

Probably designed by Gandon (1743–1823), Bishopscourt House was a porticoed residence originally built c. 1788 for the Speaker, William Lord Ponsonby, the main executive for Royal administration in the mid-eighteenth century. Its church's stone roofed chancel was the burial place of Ponsonbys and of Arthur Guinness (see Good for You, Industry, below).

CARTON HOUSE

Sometime after 1603, in an estate then known as 'Caretowne', Sir William Talbot built a Dutch-inspired winged manor house with an artificial lake supplied from waters of the River Rye. A senior judge, Richard Ingoldsby, purchased it in 1703 and added two new storeys. From 1739 it became the country seat of the FitzGeralds, Earls of Kildare and, from 1766, Dukes of Leinster. The Nineteenth Earl, Robert (1675–1744), was Lord Justice in 1714 when he engaged Richard Castle (Cassels) to redesign the house. The reconstruction included a Chinese room and a gold and white saloon featuring spectacular baroque plaster work by the Francini brothers, Paul and Philip. Richard Morrisson (1767–1849) carried out interior work at the beginning of the nineteenth century. In 1897, Queen Victoria (1819–1901) spent a night in Carton.

CASTLEMARTIN HOUSE

The U-shaped Castlemartin House near Kilcullen was built in 1730, preserving remains of a fourteenth century FitzEustace castle and chapel. Features of the estate include an avenue of lime trees, a pedimented doorway, an icehouse, tomb fragments and fine wrought iron gates. General Dundas (see Gibbet Rath, Chapter 6) made the house his headquarters.

CASTLETOWN HOUSE

'The most remarkable thing going on' in 1722, according to the philosopher George Berkeley (1685–1753), was 'a house of Mr Conolly's [at Castletown, Celbridge]. It is 142 feet in front and above 60 in the clear; the height will be about 70. It is to be of fine wrought stone.'[3]

Alessandro Galilei, who designed the façade of Saint John Lateran in Rome, was architect for the richest commoner in Ireland, William Conolly MP (1662–1729), who was Speaker of the Irish Parliament and for a time Commissioner of the Revenue. Galilei left the country and the architect of Dublin's Parliament House, Sir Edward Lovett Pearse, completed the interior. In 1740, Lady Conolly of Castletown House began erecting the obelisk-crowned arch known as 'Conolly's Folly', allegedly to relieve distress after a minor famine. Richard Castle (Cassells) may have been its architect. She built the 'Wonderful Barn' three years later for the same reason. This domed structure has five storeys and goods were hauled up through central openings in the floors.

Members of the Conolly family owned Castletown House until Mr Desmond Guinness acquired it for the Irish Georgian Society in 1965. Since 1979, it has been the property of the Castletown Foundation.

CELBRIDGE ABBEY

The Lord Mayor of Dublin, Bartholomew Van Homrigh, compatriot of William III, began building Celbridge Abbey in 1690 and he completed it in 1697. His daughter Esther (Vanessa, 1688–1723) fashioned its gardens to mark the regular visits of Jonathan Swift (1667–1745) with whom she had a difficult relationship. Lord Chief Justice Thomas Marlay lived at the Abbey after Vanessa's death. His daughter Mary was Henry Grattan's mother. Grattan claimed to have drawn inspiration from Swift and often used Vanessa's bower for composing his speeches, including his 'Declaration of Rights' in 1780.

One of Vanessa's suitors was the local vicar, Arthur Price, who, in about 1724, built the house opposite the abbey at various times called Oakley Hall, Oakley Park, Celbridge Hall, Celbridge House or Celbridge Abbey. It became the home of the Napier family. Emily Napier, Duchess of Leinster and sister of Louisa Conolly, was Lord Edward FitzGerald's mother (see Personalities, Chapter 6). General Sir William Napier (1785–1860) was a military historian, noted for his six volume *History of the War in the Peninsula* written between 1824 and 1840. The works are based on his experiences in the Napoleonic Wars and on those given to him by Arthur Wellesley, First Duke of Wellington (1769–1852) and the French Marshal Nicolas-Jean de Dieu Soult (1769–1861).

HARRISTOWN CASTLE/HOUSE

Harristown Castle was a FitzEustace stronghold but Sir Maurice Eustace, Lord Chancellor, established Harristown House in the seventeenth century. It featured a novel artificial lake complete with a man-o'-war equipped with guns. The banking La Touches purchased the estate in about 1768. William George La Touche (1747–1803) founded the first Dublin Bank and John La Touche, an Irish MP during the 1780s–90s, was a Director of the Bank of Ireland.

LYONS HOUSE

South-east of Straffan is the late eighteenth century Lyons House. Originally an Aylmer seat, Lord Cloncurry later resided there. Of Morrison and Grace designs, there were early nineteenth century additions. Its dining room has Gabrielli decoration and its demesne boasts the largest artificial lake in Ireland.

MOORE ABBEY

In the sixteenth century, the First Viscount Ely, Adam Loftus (Archbishop of Armagh from 1563 to 1568) built a mansion on the site of a Cistercian monastery in Monasterevin. Through marriage, it passed on to Sir Charles Moore, Sixth Earl (First Marquis) of Drogheda whose seat was at Mellifont Abbey in Co. Louth. He restructured it in Gothic style in 1767 to become Moore Hall (later Abbey).

The celebrated tenor, John McCormack (1884–1945) lived there between 1924 and 1936. Representatives of the 'Victor Talking Machine Company', for whom he cut nearly 200 records, visited. Other celebrities calling on him included broadcaster Monsignor Fulton Sheen (1895–1979) and boxer James Joseph (Gene) Tunney, 'The Fighting Marine' (1897–1978). From Moore Abbey the Sisters of Charity of Jesus and Mary currently manage services for people with mental disorders.

OTHER HOUSES

Straffan House (c. 1790) was the home of an important Clements family. Other significant eighteenth century houses were: Oldtown House, Naas (c. 1709); Furness House, Naas (c. 1731); Landenstown House, Clane, of the late Queen Anne (1665–1714) period; Newbury Hall, Carbury (c. 1765) and Killadoon, Celbridge (c. 1790).

RURAL HOUSING

The Statistical Survey of the Co. of Kildare issued by the Royal Dublin Society (c. 1834) described the dwellings of the period:

The farmhouses in general consist of a long thatched building of one storey, consisting of a large kitchen and fireplace in the centre, and lodging rooms at either end; the front door looks to the barns and stables on the right, behind which is the haggard and on the left are placed the cow and bullock houses.

RELIGIOUS STRUCTURES

A synod in Kells in 1152 divided Ireland into dioceses whose parameters are still similar. Since Saint Conleth (see Chapter 3) some twenty-five bishops had ruled Kildare. The synod shaped a number of minor sees to form the diocese of Meath, with Eleutherius O'Meehan as bishop. Finn O'Gorman, the Abbot of Newry, became bishop of Kildare in 1152. Two years previously he had compiled *The Book of Leinster*, a collection of historical tracts, tales, poems and genealogies, for Dermot MacMurrough. Forty-one bishops followed until, in 1846, Charles Lindsay died and Kildare was united with Dublin in the dioceses of Dublin, Glendalough and Kildare that the Church Temporalities Act of 1833 had envisaged. In 1976 a General Synod of the Church of Ireland transferred Meath from the province of Armagh to Dublin to create the united dioceses of Meath and Kildare. Its first bishop was Donald Arthur Richard Caird, who was transferred from Limerick. Walton Empey (1985–96) and Richard Clarke (1996–) followed.

Baptist Pastor Dunlop of Brannockstown established Ireland's first 'Churchmobile'. A converted bus, it was designed like a miniature church, complete with spire and fully fitted out for accommodating small congregations of his flock throughout Co. Kildare. It was dedicated in 1972.

Saint Laserian, also called Molaise (566–638) was the first Bishop of Leighlin. There were periods when abbots and bishops appear to have been synonymous but at least thirty-four men ruled before Dr Forstall received the administration of Leighlin in addition to Kildare. But the two sees merely shared a common boundary until the present double Roman Catholic diocese of Kildare and Leighlin with its fifty-six parishes began shaping a united history in 1678.

QUAKERS

Athy, Rathangan and Ballitore have a history of Quakers, the popular
name for the Society of Friends. The movement originated in the English
north-west during the mid-seventeenth century. Thomas Braddock (d.
1731) of Ballitore elaborated on the origin of the nickname.

> '*I went [to a meeting] and sat with them about half an hour, when the great power of
> the Lord came upon me, and make me fetch many deep sighs and groans, with tears;
> and a trembling came over my whole body . . .*'

Of 780 Quakers in Ireland in 1680 there were 295 in Leinster. Quakers
came to Athy as early as 1654 through a Weston family. Weekly
meetings began in the town in 1671. The movement spread and by the
eighteenth century families in the area called Baker, Doyle, Haughton,
Hudson, Rushworth, Shelly and Weston were members. They were
barred from government appointments and so were mainly merchants.
In 1780 a clothier, Thomas Chandlee, established a permanent house in
Meeting House Lane. Membership began dwindling at the turn of the
century and Methodists took over the building in 1812.

Tradition holds that two influential Quakers, John Barcroft (1664–
1724) and Abel Strettel (1659–1732) admired and then purchased the
Greese valley in Ballitore at the end of the seventeenth century. They
developed its woodlands and established the village and the area began
attracting fellow Quakers. Abraham Shackleton set up a boarding school
there in 1726. His father, Richard Shackleton (1643–1705) was the first
Shackleton to become a Quaker.

Rathangan also has a Quaker history, to which an old meeting house
and churchyard bear testimony.

'KELLYITES'

The sermons of an Anglican clergyman, Thomas Kelly (1769–1855),
offended his Dublin superiors so he left and formed the 'Kellyites' in
Athy and attracted fifty followers. They reverted to Anglicanism after his
death, as did others in the Portarlington, Co. Laois, and Blackrock, Co.
Dublin branches. Kelly's tracts were aimed at proselytising Roman
Catholics and he composed almost 800 hymns. These included the

popular 'The Head that Once was Crowned with Thorns' and 'We Sing of the Shepherd that Died'.

FAMINE

While the eastern portion of the county may have escaped the serious deprivation experienced elsewhere during the Great Potato Famine of 1845 to 1849, the same cannot be said for those parts of the county most distant from Dublin. In 1845, Prime Minister Sir Robert Peel's Scientific Committee described the situation in Kildare and adjoining counties as 'melancholy' with half the potato crop unfit for human consumption. A Constabulary Report of 13 November 1845 for Kildare town said 'Since the fall of rain, the crop is rapidly running to decay. The poorer classes of people are beginning to despair'. During the decade from 1841 to 1851 the county's population dropped by almost 20 per cent, but the Barony of North Salt (the Maynooth-Leixlip area) had a slight increase. The 1851 Census of Ireland illustrates the population change by Baronies during the decade.

	1841	1851	Change	% Change
Carbury	9,690	7,589	−2,101	−21.68
Clane	8,534	6,812	−1,722	−20.18
Connell	9,949	8,896	−1,053	−10.58
Ikeathy & Oughterany	6,162	5,239	−923	−14.98
Kilcullen	3,324	2,442	−882	−26.53
Kilkea & Moone	11,092	8,572	−2,520	−22.72
Naas, South	7,698	5,548	−2150	−27.93
Narragh & Reban East	7,049	5,105	−1,944	−27.58
Narragh & Reban West	9,035	8,354	−681	−7.54
Offaly East	10,584	8,899	−1,685	−15.92
Offaly West	11,213	8,930	−2,283	−20.36
Salt North	7,717	7,809	+92	+1.19
Salt South	4,252	3,602	−650	−15.29[4]

Population losses in urban areas were greatest in Castledermot which lost almost 53 per cent of its community. Naas had the smallest loss (–15.71 per cent). The three Co. Kildare Poor Law Unions dealing with famine relief were at Naas, Athy and Celbridge. Respectively, they extended into parts of Counties Wicklow, Queen's County (now Laois) and Dublin/Meath. A sizeable portion of north-west Kildare was in Offaly's (Edenderry Union) care and Baltinglass (Wicklow) and Carlow unions had responsibility for Graney and Grangeford, respectively.

Deaths in the county during the years 1842 to 1850 inclusive were: 991; 1,078; 1,160; 1,314; 1,603; 2,775; 2,486; 2,695; and 2,134.

There was a considerable volume of property sales during the famine and some landowners initiated relief schemes.

Dublin Castle's Outrage Papers recorded the death of a Limerick man who remained abandoned in Kildare town in the summer of 1847. After his death, an inquest attributed it to 'a Visitation of God hurried on by the total neglect of the Relief Committee, the Chairman having been informed of the deceased being exposed and lying sick in the town or street ... on Thursday 1st July 1847'.[5]

FENIAN

John Devoy (1842–1928) was the son of a labouring smallholder from Kill. He served in the French Foreign Legion before returning to Ireland to take charge of the Fenian movement within the British Army. After his arrest in 1866 he served five years of a fifteen-year sentence and obtained release on condition that he would reside outside the United Kingdom. In New York he became a Clan na Gael leader and made secret visits to Ireland. He led the celebrated *Catalpa* rescue of six Fenian prisoners from Fremantle, Australia and founded and edited the *Irish Nation* and Gaelic American publications. He spearheaded United States fundraising and helped procure arms for the 1916 Rebellion.

Among those with whom he differed were New York's Judge Daniel Cohalan (1865–1946) and Éamon de Valera (1882–1975). He supported the Anglo-Irish Treaty of 1921 and was feted at the Táiltean Games of 1924. He wrote *The Land of Éire* (1882), *The Irish Land League* (1882) and *Recollections of an Irish Rebel* (1929).

LAND LEAGUE

After the Famine, two-thirds of the land in Co. Kildare was devoted to outdoor stock-fattening and almost half of the remainder produced hay for winter feeding. There was little tillage, except in the south of the county where Athy had a significant grain industry. A third of the holdings were less than five acres. Athy Poor Law Guardians and Maynooth College authorities were among objectors to the 'Leinster Lease'—an attempt by the Duke of Leinster to prevent the compensation of tenants carrying out improvements or being disturbed. Despite this, in Co. Kildare, Michael Davitt's (1846–1906) anti-landlords movement, the Irish National Land League, was strongest among urban communities.

John Heffernan, a Kildare town merchant who also farmed fifteen acres, formed the county's first branch in March 1880. With his brother Charles, he had earlier spearheaded the local Amnesty Association for the release of Fenian prisoners. Their late father, Thomas Heffernan, had farmed fifty-six acres, had owned twenty-one cottages in Kildare and attended hunt meets and balls. John Heffernan assisted the 1880 election campaigns of the sitting MP Charles Meldon (Naas) and tenant farmer James Leahy. He made connections that proved useful the following year when a modified Coercion Act began targeting individuals, and he was arrested. A Naas solicitor, Stephen Brown, defended him, and seven years later helped Heffernan become Secretary of Kildare County Council. John Heffernan's co-initiator of the Land League branch was an Irish-American organiser, Michael Boyton.

Land agitation, including intimidation of landlords and agrarian crime, became intermittent. Michael Davitt attended a large meeting in the Curragh. In 1881, Michael Boyton was arrested in Kerry and brought to Kilmainham Jail. A March meeting of the Land League included Catholic and Protestant clergy from Kildare, Milltown and Allen, all urging moderation. John Heffernan demanded comfortable homes for labourers and their families. He also denounced the man he had helped elect, Charles Meldon MP, alleging his abandonment of League objectives. June 1881 saw Dr Kavanagh, Parish Priest of Kildare, elected President. Heffernan remained secretary and also took over Boyton's organisational duties. But the Land Act of that year, bolstered by the Arrears Act of 1882, appeased tenants sufficiently to introduce a hiatus in agrarian strife inside and outside Co. Kildare. When Charles Stewart

Parnell was released from prison in May 1882 he set about terminating the Land League. At the end of 1908 James Larkin (1876–1947) established the Irish Transport and General Workers' Union (ITGWU).

RACING ROYALS

During his second visit to Ireland, King Edward VII attended Punchestown Races on Tuesday and Wednesday, 26 and 27 April 1904. His queen, Alexandra, accompanied him and the people of Naas went to extraordinary trouble to greet them. Switzers of Dublin fashioned arches across the streets and draped a Royal Coat of Arms on the courthouse. The Urban District Council reminded citizens that His Majesty was arriving in Nás na Rí, or Naas of the Kings. They festooned the town with Union bunting and sprinkled water on the streets to dampen down the dust. The royal party arrived by train to a waiting coach each day. Bands played and crowds cheered as their entourage made its way through the town and on to the races. Representing the UDC, a Mr Staples was in position to read an address of welcome, but the King looked bored and did not stop.

FURTHER FARMING STRIFE

A 1919 campaign involving agricultural workers began in Co. Kildare when sixty labourers in Celbridge, all members of the Co. Kildare Farmers' Association, went on strike. Their employers threatened a general lockout if work did not resume immediately. In the face of this threat the ITGWU coordinated a strike throughout the county that soon spread to Co. Meath. In July 1919 the trade union pioneer and anti-conscription activist, William O'Brien (1881–1968), said 'All over the country, agricultural workers are now threatening for demands to be made on their behalf. In some counties, for instance Meath and Kildare, the war is already on.'[6] Offending farms were blockaded and strikers wielding clubs prevented the movement of goods, boycotted urban suppliers of farm owners, disrupted fairs and auctions, engaged in cattle drives and damaged crops. In response, the Irish Farmers Union attempted to employ ex-soldiers. The ploy met with little success and the Kildare Farmers' Association and the strikers agreed to settlement terms on 23 August.

HORSES AND SOLDIERS

Agriculture, waterways and the bogs contribute largely to the character of Co. Kildare (see Industry, below) but horses and the soldiers have a special association with it. Not just racehorses, whose prominence came mainly in the twentieth century. Earlier, in 1870, there was an average of 1.36 horses per household. That was high when the figure for cattle (mostly for beef) was 8.98 and for sheep, 15.01. The statistic for horses incorporated a large number of hunting and hacking animals. The Kildare Hunt, known as the 'Killing Kildares' had over sixty members in 1760.

CURRAGH CAMP

Prior to extensive roadmaking, the Curragh plain covered 1,971 hectares. The Curragh of Kildare Act of 1868 divided it into 'Brown Lands' containing the military camp whose rifle ranges were on 'Blue Lands'. The residual 'Green Lands' were for grazing and contained part of the ancient road known as Slighe Dhála Meic Umhóir (see Roadways, Chapter 2) A Curragh Ranger supervised the area from the mid-seventeenth century until 1961.

Like nearby Allen, the Curragh has associations with the legendary Fionn Mac Cumhaill and his Fianna warriors, and has historic links with armies since the arrival of the Anglo-Normans in the twelfth century. Military encampments were located there from the eighteenth century. Internal security and exigencies of the Crimean War (1853–56) necessitated a build-up of troops, and in 1855 the British army began building a permanent camp on the plain. It developed into its main Irish training centre. Queen Victoria's eldest son, Edward, Prince of Wales served in the Curragh. In 1861, the Queen visited the camp and watched him 'perform manfully the subordinate duties of a company officer in a force of some 10,000 men'. On 16 September 1861 he visited the Hill of Allen to look at work on the building of its tower. A mason, William Gorry reported:

> The Prince took out a black scut of a pipe with a shank half the length of his finger and a pouch. Two officers were along with himself, and they smoked and sung. The Prince asked me who was getting it built and I said Sir Jarald [Sir Gerald G. Aylmer, Eighth Baronet of Donadea Castle 1798–1878] One of the officers gave me a shilling. The Prince did not give anything. The Prince forgot his silver matchbox on the stone table and I kept it and had it for a long time, but someone took it off me.[7]

Besides smoking and singing, while in the Curragh the Prince arranged the smuggling in of the Dublin actress, Nellie Clifden, into the officers' mess where he was quartered.

Tℏe WREN

During that period, similar needs of other ranks were supplied on Saint Brigid's plains by an extraordinary group of females known collectively as 'The Wren of the Curragh'. In 1864, an account of their activities appeared in an article titled 'Stoning the Desolate' in the 26 November issue of the periodical *All the Year Round* 'conducted by Charles Dickens'. It described a Newbridge priest furiously knocking down one of the unfortunate women before 'tearing off her back the thin shawl . . . and with his heavy riding whip, flogging her over her bare shoulders.'

Sometimes the 'Wren' followed young men from the rural villages where they had enlisted. The wretched women lived rough among the furze bushes, particularly in the folds around Donnelly's Hollow where a tented camp was located. They burrowed away some soil, built walls and a roof with gorse and used an old sheet of corrugated iron as a door. Sods of earth kept the roof in place and a hole was left to allow the smoke from a peat fire to escape.

They 'filled the hospices with diseased and disabled soldiers' according to a contemporary account. They wore a distinctive white frieze and flannel 'Curragh Petticoat.'

'Fine-limbed, large and sturdy they were . . . well mannered when sober.' A letter written by one of them was in ' . . . as ladylike a "hand" as if it had been traced on a Davenport in Belgrave Square instead of on the bottom of a tin pot on the Curragh.' (On very cold nights the 'Wrens' took turns warming themselves by sitting on a perforated pot under which coals burned. The intruding Curragh breeze fanned the embers.)

T𝒽e 'CURRAGH INCIDENT'

The opposition of Ulster Unionists to the Third Home Rule Bill precipitated the 'Curragh Incident' (or 'Mutiny') of 1914. On 20 March, Major General Hubert Gough (1870–1963) and fifty-six of his Curragh officers offered their resignations after receiving orders to move and protect arms depots in Ulster, where officers were excused the task. Their action was successful. The War Office refused to accept their resignations and the Government allowed the Army Council to suggest that the matter was a misunderstanding. Gough, however, told the *Daily Telegraph* newspaper that he had received written guarantees of the order being revoked. He added that he would prefer to fight on behalf of Ulster than against it.

TO INDEPENDENCE AND BEYOND

VOLUNTEERS

Despite earlier strife (see Land League, above), intelligence notes from the Chief Secretary's Office in Dublin Castle from 1913 to 1916 reveal that Co. Kildare was, for the most part, 'peaceful, orderly and free from agrarian trouble'. Indeed, it 'left little to be desired' in 1913 and did not merit a separate entry. Only two 'doubtful cases' of cattle driving took place compared with nine in neighbouring Offaly. There were no cases of agitation against the grazing system.

The County Inspector of Kildare reported that there was no interest in Home Rule in Co. Kildare 'until there was a doubt about the Home Rule Bill becoming law'.[8] The Irish Volunteers that, influenced by the IRB, formed in November 1913 made little initial headway in the county whose prominent Fenian John Devoy (see above) was fund-raising in the USA. In May 1914, however, groups began drilling and membership rose to 3,000. By September 1914 the county had 32 branches and 4,492 members, only 162 of them armed. By comparison Donegal had 74 branches and 10,661 members.

That month, too, John Redmond (1856–1918) called on the Irish Volunteers to enlist and fight in the Great War of 1914 to 1918. This caused a split in the movement and those who responded to Redmond formed the National Volunteers. Roman Catholic clergy, in the main, opposed the Irish Volunteer movement and interest in it waned. Indeed, by the end of 1914 it had only 344 members in Co. Kildare, with 24 weapons.

WAR OF INDEPENDENCE

The Ancient Order of Hibernians (AOH) and the Gaelic Athletic Association (GAA) were strong in Co. Kildare at the start of 1916. Domhnal Ó Buachalla (1865–1963) from Maynooth led a local contingent to Dublin to participate in the Easter Week Rebellion (Castle Intelligence credits 'E. O'Kelly as Maynooth local organiser'[9]). He was arrested and imprisoned until the 1917 amnesty. Patrick Colgan accompanied him. Other Co. Kildare men took part in the 1916 Rebellion and some were arrested and imprisoned. Michael Smyth of Athgarvan was a typical example. He served prison terms in Richmond Barracks, Wandsworth, Wormwood Scrubs and Frongoch. He was charged with purchasing 100 rifles and 10,000 rounds of ammunition for the Irish Volunteers with £300 worth of German gold. Later, in the War of Independence, he was, in turn, adjutant of Kildare One battalion, Vice-Commandant of Kildare Two and, in 1921, Vice-Commandant of the Seventh Brigade.

Some Maynooth students supported the rebellion but, except for Father O'Brien C.C. of Kill, the clergy were outspoken in condemning it. There were no rebellion casualties in Co. Kildare. Three men were tried and imprisoned and twenty-five were arrested but released without court martial. The main effect of the rebellion occurred when the leaders were shot and recruitment for the army in the Curragh dropped.

An Athy man, Eamonn Malone, commanded the Carlow Brigade. For operational purposes, its Fifth Battalion, under J. Kavanagh, was in Athy with a company there also under Paddy Hayden. This company raided Athy Custom House and destroyed its documents. Battalion members burned an abattoir in support of the 'Belfast Boycott' of goods due to anti-Catholic rioting of 1920.

It had another company in Castledermot. The Sixth Battalion was in Suncroft with Kildare town as its F Company. Monasterevin (G) Company harassed mail trains, blocked roads and blew up bridges and culverts on main roads and Barrow crossings. Two of its members, Hugh McNally and Fintan Brennan were captured and served prison sentences. Sean Flanagan, leader of Kilrush (B) Company later became Commandant of the Sixth Battalion. This unit destroyed bridges at Kilboggan, Tippeenan and Suncroft, thus hampering troop movement from the Curragh. The company executed an alleged spy.

Most of south Kildare, therefore, was under the jurisdiction of the Carlow Brigade. A Blessington, Co. Wicklow, company drew members from east Kildare. The North Kildare Battalion was formed in Prosperous in the spring of 1917. Patrick Colgan (Maynooth) was its Commandant with Thomas Harris (Prosperous, and later a Fianna Fáil TD for the county) as his vice-commandant, Michael Smith (Athgarvan) as adjutant and Art O'Connor (Celbridge) as quartermaster. In 1920, Peadar McMahon (later Chief of Staff) came to Co. Kildare as organiser and split the North Kildare Battalion in two.

KILDARE ONE

Kildare One was under P. Colgan. P. Purcell was Vice OC. J. Fay was adjutant and P. Dunne quartermaster. It carried out assorted actions, especially against mail trains, RIC barracks and foot patrols. Being so near Dublin, it played a prominent part in security of dispatches from Volunteer GHQ in Dublin and in the interception of enemy despatches, especially to the Curragh Camp. It had two-way message-transmission centres in most of its company areas. Patrolling main roads from the city, burning records in Local Authority offices and apprehending cattle rustlers in the Curragh-Suncroft area were among its activities. A Republican Court sat at Kilgowan, Kilcullen in July 1920 where it fined and deported offenders. The Celbridge company manufactured explosives in Cauldwell's Stores and the Leixlip company fashioned land mines from cartwheels.

KILDARE TWO

Thomas Harris led Kildare Two whose headquarters was in Dowdingstown House between Athgarvan and Two-Mile-House. Michael Smith (see above) was Vice-Commandant; Sean Curry, Naas was Adjutant and Patrick Dunne, Kill, Quartermaster.

Weapons and explosives were acquired by stealth from the Curragh Camp and by raiding local houses. Incidents during the war included an attempt to blow up Limerick Bridge, Naas, the burning of RIC barracks and courthouses, destruction of British goods on trains, guarding republican court hearings and raids on mail trains. On 21 August 1920, Thomas Harris led an ambush against an RIC patrol at Greenhills, near Kill. Two policemen, Sergeant Patrick O'Reilly and Constable Patrick Flaherty (some reports say Haverty) lost their lives and some of their colleagues were injured.

After 'Bloody Sunday' (21 November 1920, when Michael Collins's 'Squad' shot dead fourteen British Secret Service Agents, provoking reprisals in Croke Park and elsewhere) there were widespread arrests throughout Co. Kildare. Thomas Harris and a number of company commanders were among those apprehended. A sympathetic RIC Sergeant McGowan and two of his constables in Newbridge alerted others, allowing them to escape.

It is worth remembering that there were military strongholds at Naas, Newbridge and the Curragh Camp. Naas RIC station was the county's Black and Tan headquarters. A Flying Column emerged in 1920, led by Martin O'Neill, which comprised personnel from counties Kildare and Wicklow. Subsequently, some of these joined the South Dublin Brigade under Gerald Boland (1885–1973) who was to become prominent in politics. There was a dispute about the ownership of their weapons and Boland alleged that it became so serious that Co. Kildare men fired on their Wicklow colleagues.

INTELLIGENCE AND INTERNMENT

Eamon Broy (1887–1972; later Colonel) from Rathangan played a critical role in the War of Independence. He was one of Collins's 'Castle Spies' and allowed Collins access to the headquarters of the Dublin Detective Force in Brunswick Street (now Pearse Street) in April 1919. He warned Collins of impending attempts to apprehend him. Arrested in March

1921, he remained in custody for four months until after the truce of 11 July. He was secretary to Collins during Treaty negotiations.

In the Curragh the detention buildings at Hare Park were full of IRA prisoners, so in 1921 the British authorities built a camp at the Gibbet Rath (Rath Camp) to house over 1,500 extra internees.

Casualties in Co. Kildare included Volunteers P. Gavin, Curragh (13 February 1919) and S. O'Sullivan, Sallins (4 May 1921). As well as the RIC casualties mentioned above (O'Reilly and Flaherty), Sergeant Joseph Hughes died in Doctor Steeven's Hospital on 21 February 1921. He had been leading a patrol of five constables in Maynooth the previous morning when they were attacked.

Cumann na mBan and Fianna Éireann were strong in both battalion areas.

NATIVE FORCES

On the morning of 16 May 1922 Lieutenant General J.J. 'Ginger' O'Connell, Deputy-Chief-of-Staff of the pro-Treaty forces took over the Curragh Camp from the departing British, and its barracks were re-named after the signatories of the Easter Week Proclamation: Pearse, McDonagh, McDermott, Clarke, Ceannt, Connolly, Plunkett. Since then the camp has been the principal training base for the Irish army. General Sean MacEoin (1893–1973), the legendary 'Blacksmith of Ballinalee' in Co. Longford was an early GOC of the camp (1925–1927). MacEoin's former Civil War field commander in the Western Command, Col Anthony Lalor was GOC in the early 1950s. The presence of the soldiers in the camp has been, under two regimes, an important factor in local economic and social affairs.

NEW STATE

After British withdrawal, Co. Kildare people began suffering from the material losses it brought. A deputation of civilians from Newbridge, Kildare and the Curragh arranged a meeting with Michael Collins, Richard Mulcahy (1886–1971) and Eamon Duggan (1874–1936) and others to discuss their predicament. A member of Kildare Co. Council, J.J. FitzGerald, pointed out that in Newbridge alone over 1,000 former civilian employees at the Curragh Camp were out of work. Collins promised that the new National Army would soon need many of them to come back and that the deputation should form a committee to establish local industries that would absorb the remainder.

CIVIL WAR

Commandant Patrick Brennan commanded the Co. Kildare Brigade of pro-Treaty sub-units during the Civil War. He deployed poorly-armed troops in Wicklow in a June 1922 attempt to isolate Dublin. The Pro-Treaty Earl of Mayo was a Senator when his Palmerstown House near Johnstown, Naas, was burned on 29 January 1923.

On the Anti-Treaty side, Co. Kildare was part of the First Eastern Division. Another Patrick (Bob) Brennan was leader and acted as officer commanding his brigade. He received assistance from Paddy Mullaney (sometimes Mullally) of Leixlip. Brennan was captured soon after the outbreak of war and Mullaney was captured after a significant confrontation on 1 December 1922. The strong Leixlip Column attacked and burned a pro-Treaty ration truck at Collinstown House, between Leixlip and Maynooth. They took the officer in charge and two men to a house at Pike Bridge and held them, then commandeered a passing car belonging to Doctor Patrick Keelan, of Mullingar. Commandant General Hogan, Brigadier McDonnell and Commandants Saurin and Travers with a Whippet armoured car went to their comrades' rescue. They surrounded the anti-Treaty troops and, after a battle lasting four hours, captured twenty-two of them with their arms. Five of these were deserters from Baldonnel Camp and they were convicted by general court martial and executed on 8 January 1923 on charges of treachery, 'in that at Leixlip [they] assisted certain armed prisoners in using force against National Troops, and [for] treacherously communicating and consorting with the armed persons mentioned.'[10] These were Terence Brady, Leo Dowling, Sylvester Heaney, Anthony O'Reilly and Laurence Sheehy.

The late Sean McBride (1904–1988) sat on an anti-Treaty court that later tried Mullally and others for signing a document promising 'not to use arms against the parliament elected by the Irish people . . .' This action averted their execution. McBride was anti-Treaty Director of Organisation. He had endured hunger strike in 1923 when imprisoned in Newbridge and escaped from custody when being transferred to Kilmainham Jail. See Appendix 2.

CIVIC GUARD

The Civic Guard, later An Garda Síochána (Guardians of the Peace), was established after the War of Independence. At a meeting in the Gresham Hotel, Dublin on 9 February 1922, the Provisional Government appointed a Police Organising Committee that included former Dublin Metropolitan Police (DMP) sergeant Eamon Broy (see War of Independence, above), and Jeremiah Maher, ex RIC sergeant of Naas who had joined the Volunteers. A force emerged and Kildare Barracks became its training depot. Dissension grew there between former RIC members who had joined the force and members recruited from those who had fought in the War of Independence. Particularly, there was resentment towards former RIC officers obtaining high rank in the new force. Senior pro- and anti-Treaty leaders became embroiled in a crisis that even a visit from Michael Collins failed to contain. It reached its climax when anti-Treaty troops raided the barracks on 17 June 1922, occupied it and removed arms and ammunition. This defiance of the Provisional Government was a significant prelude to the shelling of the Four Courts in Dublin on 28 June and it became known as the Kildare Mutiny.

ANOTHER 'MUTINY'

With the Civil War past, by March 1924 a government demobilisation plan envisaging massive reduction in the strength of the new state's army was in place. It would bring the figure from 48,176 to 15,838 within a year. Justified because the threat of war was past, the proposition was resisted fiercely. An ultimatum to the government to cease demobilisation caused a major crisis. Before it was resolved, two government ministers had resigned and a number of Army Headquarters and Curragh officers had been replaced. The affair became known as the 'Army Mutiny' or the 'Tobin Mutiny' after Major General Liam Tobin, a signatory of the ultimatum.

The EMERGENCY

Young Irishmen flocked to join the army during 'The Emergency'–the term describing the period of neutral Ireland's war years (1939–45).

Searchlight beams stabbing the night sky from the Curragh were visible across Co. Kildare. Schoolmasters sent pupils, delighted to miss classes, to obliterate the school's name with cement wash for fear that invading Germans would benefit from knowing that they were in Baile-an-tSéipéil or some such location! Careful folk observed nightly blackouts, stored coal, sugar, and tea and sieved 'black flour' through scarce silk stockings. They sang:

> Bless de Valera and Sean McEntee,
> Bless their brown bread and their half-ounce of tea.

Emergency planning earmarked Maynooth and Clongowes Wood colleges as base hospital locations in the event of an evacuation from Dublin.

In September 1939 the army mobilised with a strength of 19,136. On 20 May 1940 the Local Security Force (LSF) emerged. It was organised around Garda Síochána districts. 'A' Group was to be an auxiliary to the army and 'B' group to the Garda Síochána. In January 1941, 'A' group became the Local Defence Force (LDF) with formal military status.

INTERNEES

During 'The War' IRA prisoners were held at Number One Internment Camp ('Tintown') in the Curragh. Bernard Casey from Co. Longford died after a shooting incident there in 1940. International internees—British, Canadian, Italian, Polish, German and one American—were held in the eastern extremity of the camp. Connecting a fire engine pump to the Curragh sewerage system allegedly halted an isolated breakout attempt!

Normally, however, the regime was not strict. There was a generous system of parole based on honour and in one case a Royal Air Force pilot brought his wife over to Newbridge and lived with her there by day. These men became frequent and popular visitors to Newbridge, Kildare and Naas. They sold odd items that they had crafted in the camp to fellow customers in bars and barbers' shops. Kildare people tell many 'tall tales' around firesides about their exploits but there were as many hair-raising authentic incidents.

'Sliabh na mBan', the Whippet armoured car allocated to Michael Collins during the War of Independence, was cared for at 'Tintown' by the Cavalry Corps. During an IRA campaign of 1956 to 1959, 'Tintown' was full again and in December 1958 fifteen internees escaped. The internment camp was demolished in 1980 but the Curragh's military prison 'The Glasshouse' housed IRA prisoners in the 1970s. It later formed part of the general prison system.

A NATIVE PARLIAMENT

In the Kildare North constituency in the 1918 election for the Westminster parliament, the Sinn Féin candidate, Dómhnal Ó Buachalla, from Maynooth, beat J. O'Connor (Nationalist Party) with 68 per cent of the vote for a single seat. Kildare South also had a single seat and A. O'Connor (Sinn Féin) beat Denis Kilbride (Nationalist Party) with a massive 82 per cent of the vote. With the other Sinn Féin members elected nationwide, they entered the first Dáil Éireann that assembled at the Mansion House, Dublin on 21 January 1919.

The term 'Blueshirts' given to the National Guard, formerly the Army Comrades Association, originated in Co. Kildare, where the movement was strong. Its Fine Gael deputy, Sidney Minch, wore a blue shirt in Dáil Éireann on 17 September 1934, and the following day a number of his colleagues followed suit. The large farm owners of county Kildare were prominent in the movement and in the anti-rates campaign of that period. The movement's detractors used an intercepted letter from a Mylie Magee from Ballymore Eustace to suggest that members carried arms.

The Labour party opposed the Blueshirt movement and in due course the party flourished in Co. Kildare. William Norton (1900–1963) was an impressive politician, winning elections for over thirty years.

Co. Kildare's early electoral areas were Athy, Clane, Kildare town, Maynooth, Naas and Newbridge. There was considerable poverty in the county and agricultural matters dominated among concerns of the electorate. Farmers were demanding better returns for produce, a system of cattle testing, creameries, and, particularly on the Curragh, more sheep-dipping facilities and action against worrying from dogs. Turfcutters wanted adequate access to bogs, better turf prices, bog and river drainage. Urban folk wanted improvements in sanitation and housing. After its formation in 1926, Fianna Fáil recognised this and its strength grew as they addressed the complaints. Other issues at election times included provision of better hospital care and library facilities, public toilets and Civic Guard/Garda Siochána stations.

Dómhnal Ó Buachalla became Governor General of Saorstát Éireann, the Irish Free State (1932–37). The county elected some prominent politicians and government ministers. W. Norton (see above), Labour party leader from 1932 to 1960, was Tánaiste and Minister for Social Welfare from 1948 to 1951 and Tánaiste and Minister for Industry and Commerce from 1954 to 1957). Gerard Sweetman (1908–1970), Alan Dukes (1945–) and Charlie McCreevy (1949–) were Ministers for Finance. Dukes also held portfolios in Transport, Energy and Communications from 1996 to 1997, Justice from 1986 to 1987 and Agriculture from 1981 to 1982. He was also leader of the Fine Gael party. Paddy Power (1928–) was Minister for Fisheries and Forestry from 1979 to 1981, Minister for Defence in 1982 and an MEP from 1977 to 1979. Emmet Stagg was Minister of State at the Department of the Environment, with special responsibility for Housing and Urban Renewal from 1993 to 1994. He was also Minister of State at the Department of Transport, Energy and Communications with Special Responsibility for Nuclear Safety, Renewable Energy, Gas and Oil Industry, Air Safety, Road Haulage and Bus Regulation from 1994 to 1997. Joe Bermingham (1919–1995) was Minister of State at the Department of Finance with Responsibility for the Office of Public Works and was Chairman of the Parliamentary Labour Party from 1976 to 1986. See Appendix 3.

EUROPEAN PARLIAMENT

Patrick Power became a member of the European Parliament on the resignation of James Gibbons and David Thornley (1977 to 1979).

LOCAL GOVERNMENT

From 1838, boards of guardians became responsible for orphans and children's welfare, welfare assistance and workhouses that often functioned as hospitals. County health boards took over their duties in 1922. Celbridge workhouse closed and Athy and Naas became, respectively, the County Home and County Hospital. The Drogheda Memorial Hospital on the Curragh became known as the 'Jockey Hospital'.

A 1970 Health Act provided for the establishment of eight regional health boards with local advisory committees. Kildare, Wicklow and Dublin formed the Eastern Health Board region that later became the East Coast Area Health Board.

COUNTY COUNCIL

Kildare County Council emerged in 1899 with Stephen J. Brown of Naas as its first Chairman. He received a celebratory torchlight procession. The Council's first meeting took place in Naas Courthouse on 22 August. The first resolution adopted was 'That we affirm the right of the Irish Nation to a full measure of self-government. We accept the Local Government Act of 1898 as a first installment of the same and call on the Imperial Parliament to proceed with the further restitution of our rights.'[11]

Rural District Councils maintained roads, water supply, sanitation and housing up to 1925. Athy and Naas had Town Commissions until 1900, when they became Urban District Councils with responsibilities for housing, water, sewerage, markets, fairs, lanes and lighting within town bounds. Newbridge continued with Commissioners who had a significant role in housing. See Appendix 4.

INDUSTRY

Textiles featured prominently in early Co. Kildare industry. There were cotton mills in Prosperous and in Leixlip, where an iron mill also flourished for over a century from 1732. Ballymore Eustace had a weaving industry. Sallins and Johnstown had grain mills, Naas a woollen mill and Monasterevin a distillery, a brewery, a malthouse and a tobacco manufacturing business (See Monasterevin, Chapter 6). Later, the town had a knitwear factory.

Celbridge has its place in the world of fashion: in July 1796, the *Hull Advertiser* announced: 'The straw bonnets now so much the fashion originated in Ireland; and from a praiseworthy motive in Lady Louisa Conolly who, to employ the poor of Celbridge . . . instituted a manufacture of straw into hat and bonnets, which rapidly improved and gave bread to hundreds. Females were the manufacturers.'

Kilcock had six distilleries in the eighteenth century. Athy has always had an association with malting, print and timber products. The Ballysax (Curragh) Brick and Tile Company opened in 1903 and closed in 1932 after intermittent output.

For many years Kildare town had the only wallpaper factory in Ireland and Black and Decker Ireland later produced power tools there. A photography business (Polaroid) in Newbridge did not survive, but its rope factory became a lasting major concern as did its cutlery and (later) silver plants. Leixlip has become an important centre for technological research and production. In Donadea Wood during World War Two, Italians built pyres of damp wood with a central cavity into which they tossed embers. The pyre smouldered for days and eventually produced charcoal. After the war, turfcutters' hostels were vacated (see below) and a pipe factory and mushroom growing operation used the accommodation for a while. Work on the Golden Falls hydro-electric plant at Leixlip began in 1946, and Allenwood had a peat-generated power station (see Turf [Peat] below).

RURAL ELECTRIFICATION

Nicholas Callan's (see Maynooth College, above) enormous contribution to electrical science was an important early step towards bringing electricity to Irish homes. The Dublin Electric Light Company had seventeen electric arc lamps in operation by 1831. In 1889 Carlow became the first provincial town to have public electric lighting. Within a decade Kildare followed suit. It would be some time, however, before country cottages would leave behind their paraffin lamps.

Ireland's Rural Electrification Scheme began in 1946 and Co. Kildare's first area to benefit was Kill. Work began there in 1948. Soon parish priests were holding switching-on ceremonies in village halls throughout the county and one old lady in Clane parish asked 'how did they get up there to light it?'. Kildangan proved troublesome, where 196 of its 509 premises were labourers' cottages. Of these, 109 felt that their landlords should pay for wiring expenses, particularly since they had only part-time employment. Diplomacy eventually resolved the situation. Experiments in providing concrete piles instead of wooden poles for carrying electricity took place in Ballitore. They gave excellent service, but cost and transportation difficulties ruled out more extensive use.

AGRICULTURE

There are records of harvest failures in Co. Kildare in 1525, from 1629 to 1633, and in 1708. These occurred long before the potato famines of the 1840s (see Famine, above). Its rich soil made Co. Kildare an agricultural county and its farmers had some of the largest holdings in the country (see Land League, above). The county has prime fattening land and the Curragh has a long tradition of sheep grazing. Kildare farmers also practise dairy farming and pig and poultry raising. Compulsory tillage during World War Two added to the number of farms growing cereal crops.

In 1940 Kildare led the country's list of large farms. Farm sizes were: up to 30 acres, 9 per cent; 30–50 acres, 8 per cent; 50 to 100 acres, 16 per cent; 100–200, 26 per cent; over 200, 41 per cent. During an outbreak of foot and mouth disease in 1941, soldiers from the Curragh dug huge trenches on farms before shooting and burying valuable herds across the county.

In the new millennium, estimates put the gross agricultural output from 3,000 farming families at €160m. Adding direct payments and subsidies, this would represent over €200m. Diversification has become necessary, however, and horticulture has been developing rapidly. Its produce includes vegetables, mushrooms, flowers, bulbs and other nursery products. Imaginative farming methods such as deer and ostrich farming are also in evidence. An English-born couple inherited a farm in Carbury and began breeding alpacas, despite a £10,000 price tag on a pregnant female. Weighing 4.5 kilogrammes, the first Kildare-born alpaca was born in the autumn of 2001. The annual Kildare Co. Show provides an overview of farming successes.

TURF (PEAT)

As early as 1825 there was discussion on the possibility of exploiting peat as a source of fuel, but attempts to advance the notion received little encouragement from the establishment. Paper manufactured from peat was produced in 1835 and from 1839 to 1848 Wye Williams of the City of Dublin Steam Packet Company used hydraulic presses and other paraphernalia to produce coke from peat in Kilcock. Between 1903 and 1905, the Callender Company in Celbridge produced postcards and wrapping paper from a mixture of moss peat and paper pulp. Ree Reece's Irish Peat Company distilled peat to produce candle wax at Kilberry, Athy, from 1849 to 1859.

Charcoal was also an early bog product. In 1850, Jasper Rogers and the Irish Amelioration Society began producing peat charcoal at Derrymullan, near Robertstown. According to Rogers (whose enthusiasm led him to name his Robertstown home 'Peat House'), one of its aims was the provision of employment for 'miserable and half-starved spectres who inhabited this dreary waste'. His society envisaged a depot situation for receiving all hand-won turf from Kildare bogs. This, they felt, would improve standards of living. Because of an insufficient market for charcoal, the enterprise only survived for seven years.

By this time, the Irish Peat Company was manufacturing peat briquettes at Kilberry (1855–58). A more elaborate briquette operation began at Derrylea, near Monasterevin, in the 1860s but, like a neigbouring project to fuel railway locomotives with turf, it was short lived. A retired British army major (McQuaid) began manufacturing peat litter and firelighters at Umeras, Monasterevin, in 1890. Under different managements it survived for half a century. As noted above, Celbridge manufactured peat fibres in the early twentieth century.

In 1917, the government set up a Peat Committee which produced a positive report, but the prevailing political climate prevented its receiving any priority. The following year a Mr F.A. Evans began producing peat moss at Mulgeeth, Carbury, but his enterprise failed after two years.

Native government realised the potential of the country's vast area of bogland, however, and in 1933 Doctor C.S. 'Todd' Andrews (1901–1985) became an official of the Department of Industry and Commerce charged with turf development. Andrews had gone on hunger strike, had tunnelled out of the Curragh internment camp in 1921, and had also been interned there in 1923/1924. Now he was back studying the Co. Kildare countryside and continued doing so until 1958, when he became Chairman of Córas Iompair Éireann (CIÉ).

He initiated a new section within the Department of Industry and Commerce to promote the production and marketing of hand-won turf through cooperative turf societies. These societies received engineering advice from the County Council's County Surveyor. A Turf Development Board emerged in 1934 to carry out studies into uses for milled peat as operated on the continent.

PLAN ONE

Its Plan One was accelerated with the advent of war. World War Two brought the rationing of food and clothing and a shortage of coal. Turf was suddenly an important commodity, although passengers on trains run on wet sods experienced long delays. Well-dressed city business-men walked through Co. Kildare farmyards, trying to keep their spats in pristine condition as they bargained with turfmen. Lines of carts set off for the city daily. Manzor's of Clane was a popular early-morning stop for breakfast; cheese and onion sandwiches with porter for the drivers and nosebags full of oats for the horses. Large amounts of cash received in Dublin crossed the counter at the 'Deadman's' pub in Palmerstown on the way home and many horses found their own way as their masters lay asleep in their carts.

Dublin needed fuel and the Turf Development Board went into large-scale production to supply large stacks of the black or brown 'gold' in the Phoenix Park. It is estimated that over 500,500 tons were delivered between 1942 and 1947. The army operated a turf camp at Coolcarrigan.

There was a shortage of local labour in Co. Kildare so hostels, better known as Turf Camps, were built in Corduff South (or Timahoe South), Corduff Middle and Mucklon. There were other operations in Allenwood, Ballydermot, Drummond, Kilberry, Lullymore and Robertstown. 'Westerns', mostly from Co. Mayo, occupied the hostels. They moved about in open lorries and whistled at shy country lasses whose smaller siblings sneaked into the Sunday 16mm film shows in the camps, hoping their parents would not find out.

A peat milling plant at Lullymore began producing briquettes in 1934. The Turf Development Board acquired it in 1940 and increased its production. Carbury Peat Fuel Company was milling peat from 1935. It went into liquidation in 1939 and the Turf Development Board took over its assets and operations the following year. The Board had a research and experimental station and central stores complex in Newbridge. Kilberry produced peat moss, mainly for export. Under the Turf Development Act of 1946 the Board became Bord na Móna.

PLAN TWO

The major undertaking of Plan Two was Allenwood power station. It was established as a joint venture between Bord na Móna and the ESB. Pranksters topping off its cooling tower tossed down a dummy, causing consternation among onlookers. An area of bog was developed especially for supplying the pilot milled peat boiler at the station. The station provided electricity until its demolition in 1997.

The Turf Development Act of 1950 initiated the building of villages for Bord na Móna employees. Co. Kildare's main complex was at Coill Dubh (Blackwood, Timahoe) where 146 houses were constructed.

At Allenwood in the 1950s, a French-run concern, Irish Ceca Ltd. produced charcoal from turf for use in the purification of foodstuffs and chemicals.

At the close of the twentieth century Bord na Móna was marketing 3.5 million tonnes of milled peat, 41,000 tonnes of sod peat and 276,000 tonnes of peat briquettes, as well as horticultural growing media. Its annual turnover was IR£66.27m. It then had two main components: Bord na Móna Environmental Ltd and Bord na Móna PLC (with subsidiaries in fuels, horticulture, briquettes and machine turf).

The Irish Peatland Conservation Council (IPPC) keeps a watchful eye on areas listed under a number of environmental, natural heritage, biogenetic, special protection and other categories. They include bogs and fens at Ardkill, Ballynafagh, Blackwood, Cappagh, Carbury, Derryvullagh, Hodgestown, Leixlip (Louisa Bridge) Lullymore (Lodge), Mouds, Pollardstown, Món Rúadh, the River Barrow, Rye Water Valley-Carton and Usk marshes.

Kildare people recall families working on the bog, the father working the strap socket slean associated with the county, the mother arriving with the meals and, at a later stage, joining the children in 'footing' the sods for drying.

Bog historians reckon that a Lullymore man, Christy Daly, was the fastest sleansman who ever worked anywhere. He cut 100 sods per minute and cleared 598.5 cubic metres in forty-eight man-hours. An observer who watched him in 1945 said the sods were touching each other as they flew from the bog-hole and that it took six 'catchers' and 'wheelers' to remove his output.

HORSE RACING, TRAINING AND BREEDING

The Curragh has been the premier racecourse in Ireland since the seventeenth century, and it remains the home of the Irish Classics. Punchestown has been celebrated as the location of the Co. Kildare Hunt Races since 1850. Schools once closed during the races because it had a carnival atmosphere that delighted young and old. That course now has more than an annual meeting, and also hosts trials and eventing.

British Hussars once provided mounted 'sweepers' to clear the public from the racecourse at the two venues. From the formation of the new state, the Artillery Corps, stationed at McGee Barracks, Kildare and riders of the horse transport branch of the Supply and Transport corps on the Curragh continued the practice at both venues. They now appear at Punchestown alone, where an Army hospitality marquee is also a feature.

Naas also has a fine racecourse that features both flat and hurdle events.

Colonel William Hall-Walker was a member of a Scottish brewing family. In 1900, he purchased a farm at Tully, outside Kildare town, and began breeding horses. He also conceived the Japanese Gardens with horticultural, artistic, religious, historical and philosophical influences. He engaged Japanese gardener Tassa Eida and his son Minoru to complete the landscaping. The Irish National Stud Company Ltd., established in 1945, began operating the stud a year later with a primary aim of promoting the interest of the bloodstock industry, using high-class stallions. Now totalling 347 hectares, the operation includes a horse museum (containing the skeleton of the celebrated racehorse Arkle) and its Japanese Gardens have become world famous. Saint

Fiachra's Commemorative Garden, created in 1999 to celebrate the approaching millennium, was designed by Professor Martin Hallinan.

Bloodstock is a major industry in Co. Kildare. Equestrian and dressage centres, livery yards, breeding and training establishments employ large numbers, and legendary trainers include people like Paddy ('Darkie') Prendergast, the first Irish trainer to head the British Trainers' Table.

Racehorses have made names too, and not always for winning races. On 8 February 1983 the record-breaking Shergar disappeared from the Aga Khan's Ballymany Stud, outside Newbridge, days before his second season at stud was due to begin. The horse has never been seen since.

Jockeys whose names remain synonymous with Kildare racing include Aubrey Brabazon, Joe Canty, Morny Wing, Martin Moloney, Pat and Toss Taaffe. The National Stud (Kildare), the Aga Khan Stud (Newbridge) and Goff's Bloodstock Sales (Kill) have international standing.

Sales and services concerns connected with the industry are located at Monasterevin, Donadea, Clane, Kill and Kildare. Berney Brothers Ltd continue an old family saddling and harness-making tradition in Kilcullen. For decades, travellers through the town watched out for the horse in their shop window.

The headquarters of the Turf Club is at the Curragh Racecourse. Its registry office administers the rules of racing in respect of all forms of flat and steeplechasing, including point-to-point racing. It issues licences for trainers, jockeys and other participants in racing.

The racing in county men's blood has spread abroad too. Kevin Connolly began his career with his trainer father, Michael, in his Kildare town home. After gaining experience in Macau and Australia, he established the Tongshun Jockey Club in Beijing in 2001, when gambling was still illegal in China.

QUARRYING

The giant Cement Roadstone Holdings corporation quarries on the Hill of Allen. The Kildare Environmental Circle and VOICE (Voice of Irish Concern for the Environment) have been protesting against the work. After over fifty years a considerable portion of the west face of the historic hill has been removed.

GOOD FOR YOU

Ireland's best-known citizen was born in Celbridge. Arthur Guinness (1725–1803) was the eldest son of Richard Guinness, agent and receiver for Doctor Arthur Price, Archbishop of Cashel, later Bishop of Meath. Tradition has it that young Arthur helped his father brew table-beer in Celbridge for Doctor Price's use. In 1756, Arthur leased a brewery in Leixlip, where the water was said to have enhanced his product. In 1759 he began brewing at Saint James's Gate, Dublin, and the rest is history– and more!

Guinness had expressed opposition to the United Irishmen in their 1798 rebellion, and so his brew was initially called 'Guinness's black Protestant porter'. He is buried in a church on the Bishopscourt House estate at Oughterard, near Kill.

AIR RAISING

Captain Darby Kennedy established Weston Ltd airport near Leixlip in the late 1940s. His 1936 De Havilland Dragon, EI-AFK, was a familiar sight in the county's skies for sixteen years as he flew charter and sightseeing trips. In 1967 it became the *Iolar*, the first Aer Lingus aircraft and ceremoniously led in the company's first jumbo jet after its 1971 touchdown in Dublin airport. Weston played a significant role in the development of Irish aviation.

LEISURE AND TOURISM

For modern tourism management and promotion, Co. Kildare lies in the East Coast & Midlands Tourism region. County Kildare Fáilte Ltd provides an on-the-spot service to tourism from its offices and through www.kildare.ie. The main towns have heritage or information centres. Those in Kildare town and Athy are particularly well developed. The county's tourist attractions range from a butterfly farm in Straffan to canal barge hire in Athy. Historic houses remain open to the public and angling, golf, horseracing, country rambles and cycle routes, gardens, equestrian centres, forest parks, historic sites, and arts and crafts are all popular. The Barrow navigation has over 192 kilometres of cruising waterways that also offer canoeing, angling and other water sport opportunities.

AGENCIES AND SMALL INDUSTRIES

The Kildare County Development Board was established in March 2000 to coordinate agencies and interests involved in developing the county's economic, social and cultural enterprises. It has a Community and Enterprise office in the County Council buildings in Naas. Kildare County Enterprise Board is housed in Clane. 'Kildare 2012' is the Board's Ten Year Strategy for Economic, Social & Cultural Development. It aims at fostering cooperation so that Co. Kildare will offer an improved environment in which to live, work, visit and do business.

ASK (Action South Kildare) was formed in 1993 to tackle long term unemployment and social disadvantage in the south Kildare area. It is a community-based local development company that co-ordinates the efforts of state bodies, the local authority, voluntary agencies, local communities and willing entrepreneurs for the benefit of the south Kildare area. It focuses particularly on training, childcare, education, enterprise, homelessness, drugs awareness, community development and Traveller issues.

KELT (Kildare European Leader II Teóranta) is based in Clane. It was established in 1995 and is funded by the European Union to promote and fund rural development within Co. Kildare. Originally established to administer the Leader II programme, it took on the operation of the Leader Plus programme in Co. Kildare for the period 2002–2006. Under this programme, KELT has the authority to distribute a total of €5,115,000 to eligible innovative community and private sector projects.

OAK (Offaly and Kildare) was formed in 1995 to encourage communities and individuals to achieve their potential by challenging economic and social disadvantage and address problems in north Offaly and north-west Kildare.

Co. Kildare Library and Arts Service in Newbridge has a History and Family Research Centre.

Co. Kildare's small or craft industries include: crochet; knitwear; jewellery; wood sculptures; lace; stained glass at Celbridge; yarns at Johnstown; pottery at the Curragh and Moone; forged ironwork at Athy; heraldic crafts at Kildare; pewter and jewellery at Timolin; woodturning at Carbury and Castledermot; ceramics at Ballymore Eustace; ogham and art copper at Straffan; and woollens at Kildare. Customers from far beyond the county have worn the celebrated handmade shoes from Tutty's of Naas and, more recently, Peacockes of Kilcullen.

SPORT

From 1740 until 1951, the 'Fair of the Furze' took place between Maddenstown and French Furze on the Curragh. It featured a form of hurling between Co. Kildare men from either side of the Liffey. There were no medals, just a barrel of porter and tobacco-packed pipes for the victors. Wrestling on the side-line was a common feature of early games.

South Co. Kildare was cock-fighting country. It took place in most villages, particularly around Athy, from the seventeenth to the twentieth centuries. Even the Quaker village of Ballitore had a pit for the cruel contests. The *Leinster Leader* of 30 September 1916 reported that 1,000 spectators attended a fight at Kilrush when two doctors, two solicitors and three members of the Athy Board of Guardians were arrested for alleged involvement.

The eighteenth century practice of bull baiting took place at Naas Market Cross. Archibald Hamilton Rowan of Rathcoffey described the early blood sport as:

> *An innocent and manly amusement for the lower ranks of people [in which] a bull is procured, the wilder the better for the sport, and fastened to a stake by a rope about ten yards long in any commodious place. The spectators make a ring around him, the hardiest in the front, as their duty is when a dog is thrown up into the air, to run within the ring and by catching him to prevent him receiving any injury from the fall. The bull's horns seldom pierce the skin of the dog, but it frequently happens that men are hurt. Each person possessed of a dog brings him on a chain; there are never more than two, and generally one dog let on the bull at the time. Should a dog attack a bull anywhere but in front, he is taken up and turned out of the ring. That dog acquires the greatest favour who most frequently pins the bull, that is, seizes him*

by the upper lip, between the nostrils, and that man who has caught the most dogs has plainly been the most intrepid.[12]

At the end of the frolics, the bull was slaughtered and the flesh was distributed to the destitute. At the last baiting in Naas the beast tossed a cavalryman in the air and went berserk through the streets until a pursuer stabbed it in Basin Lane. The pastime warranted an appalling stage-Irish ballad in *Pat Connor's Song Book*:

> *Myself, Pat O'Tullomagh came from Kildare.*
> *Whack, and old Erin, for ever, O!*
> *For jigging a lilt was the boy to a hair*
> *And at bull-baiting, monstrous clever, O!*
> *And arrah, and why not?*
> *'Tis a way we have got*
> *To make the time pass away gaily, O.*
> *But, though Bulls, we avow,*
> *It isn't easy to cow*
> *The lads of the land of shillelah, O!*[13]

PITCH-AND-TOSS

During the first half of the twentieth century men in navy Sunday suits attended 'pitch-and-toss schools' at crossroads and street corners throughout Co. Kildare. If the two pennies tossed in the air from a comb or a piece of wood came down 'heads' or 'tails' the manipulator won. Other bets were laid on a 'pitcher' landing his coin nearest a stone marker.

GAELIC GAMES

Hurling takes second place to Gaelic football in Co. Kildare, where gambling and Gaelic football can arouse passion. These sporting inclinations were united for a brief spell in the 1940s when a greyhound-racing track was laid about the Sarsfields GAA pitch in Newbridge, to the chagrin of the Central Council of that body. A ban on foreign games was in force and the patriotism of dogs was open to question! The Kildare county team boldly broke with tradition by interfering for the first time with their pristine strip. Emblazoned on their 'lilywhite' breasts were defiant red hounds.

Long before designer kit became obligatory, young boys pulled 'crooky sticks' from hedges to hurl in playgrounds or kicked about an inflated pig's bladder in a rushy field after completing homework in the evenings. Larry Stanley, Matt Goff, Paul Doyle—great names from a glorious sporting past—dropped from lips as easily as fondly-remembered horses like Tulyar, Brown Stout and Caughoo (accused of hiding in gorse bushes during a foggy Irish Grand National and popping out fresh and able to finish well ahead of the field next time around).

The county won the All-Ireland Gaelic Football Championship in 1905, 1919, 1927 and 1928. The players developed a fast, short hand-passing style and were the first to win the Sam Maguire Cup by defeating Cavan in 1928. The county has never captured the GAA grail since. Before the 1935 semi-final the team became the first to engage in collective training. This was repeated for the final amid disapproval from purists. The training took place at Oakley Park, Celbridge, and there were reports of sessions in more than hand-passing! Other complaints included the exorbitant cost of the exercise and the unexpected dropping of star goalkeeper Patrick 'Chuddy' Chanders of Athy just before the final. Kildare lost to Cavan (2–5 to 3–6) and left the All-Ireland stage for many decades.

'LILYWHITES'

The origin of the term 'Lilywhites' is obscure. Folklorists say that the legendary cloak of Saint Brigid that spread across the Curragh (see Chapter 3) was white and that Co. Kildare people received the nickname as a result. Some sport historians offer a theory that the county supported the Yorkists who wore white roses in the Wars of the Roses (1455–1485). Others say the term originated later when the support was for King James II (1633–1701) whose troops wore the white cockade. In 1797, Lord Edward FitzGerald is alleged to have attended a match between Kildare and Meath in which Kildare wore white linen shirts. When Cumann Luthcleas Gael (Gaelic Athletic Association [GAA]) was formed in 1884, counties normally wore the colours of their champion club, so Kildare wore the green and black hooped jerseys of Clane William O'Brien club (these later became Johnstown Bridge's colours). Clane changed their club colours to white (some say they initially borrowed white rugby jerseys from Clongowes Wood College). The county team wore the Clane colours in the triple All-Ireland final against Kerry in 1903 that they lost, 0–8 to 0–2. They even dyed their boots white. Clane and Co. Kildare have worn white ever since.

Football lore also suggests that Clane women sewed up flour bags to make the kit. 'Come on the flour bags' was a common taunt to young men who togged out behind hedges each Sunday. Kilcullen footballers suffered from a similar malign tale that gave them the nickname 'The Rags'.

Saint Mary's, Leixlip, included two of Co. Kildare's early stars, Larry Stanley and Matt Goff. Paul Doyle of Suncroft was another outstanding player and years after the county's All-Ireland successes he regaled many a young soldier in the Curragh's Sandes Home with stories of great encounters. Later, legendary goalkeeper Tommy Malone of Carbury, 'Boiler' White and Micky Geraghty of Sarsfields (Newbridge), Bob Martin (Eadestown), Jim Daly, (Cappagh), 'Kaiser' Bracken, Clane, and Davy Dalton (Kilcock) were county players of note. With the advent of the 'All Stars' awards, players honoured included O. Crinnigan (1978), M. Lynch (1991), N. Buckley, D. Dalton, G. Ryan, (1997) G. Ryan, B. Lacey, J. Finn (1998), K. O'Dwyer, D. Earley (1999), A. Rainbow (2000).

Desperate because of their years in the wilderness, a well-funded supporters' club emerged to back the team financially. Mick O'Dwyer of Kerry became coach. The strategy succeeded and supporters of the 'short grass county' who had remained among the most loyal in the country enjoyed watching the team improve. Then came a highly-charged year in 1998. Kildare reached the All-Ireland final and the county went berserk. White tractors and carts appeared on roadsides and white flags were everywhere—even over some graves in Newbridge cemetery. Kildare played splendidly in the first half of the match but Galway emerged invigorated after the interval and won by sixteen points to two goals and five points.

In 2001, RTÉ attempted to capture the passion of Co. Kildare club football in a television drama series called 'On Home Ground'. Shot on location in Kilcock and the surrounding area, the fictitious village was called Kildoran.

RACING

See Horse Racing, Training and Breeding in Industry, above. Greyhound racing has a large following on Mondays and Fridays at Newbridge track.

MOTOR RACING

Racing cars painted in national colours sped along Co. Kildare roads at over eighty miles per hour on 2 July 1903. The first Gordon Bennett motor race had taken place three years previously from Paris to Lyons. Tycoon newspaper owner and international exploration and sports patron James Gordon Bennett (1841–1918) was the sponsor. It lasted until 1905 and was a seminal series that led to Grand Prix racing. The 1903 circuit of 100 miles embraced the towns of Co. Kildare, Kilcullen, Monasterevin and Athy. It included a treacherous bend at the Moat of Ardscull. Camille Jenatzy, a Belgian driving for Germany, won the race in a Mercedes.

Straffan was the home of one of Ireland's most celebrated sportsmen, the motorcyclist Stanley Woods. He won ten Tourist Trophy races in the Isle of Man. Car races and motor-cycle 'scrambles' were popular on the Curragh before Mondello Park, at Donore, near Naas, became a modern performance driving circuit.

GOLF

A feature in *The Field* of 11 September 1875 told of 'days of yore, when His Excellency the Earl of Eglinton [1812–1862] played a round' on the Curragh golf links with the officer commanding the Queen's Boys Regiment that was posted to Newbridge Barracks in 1852. The course was near Donnelly's Hollow. In 1910 it became the 'Royal Curragh', but the appendage disappeared after the War of Independence.

The County Kildare Golf Club outside Naas evolved, apparently, between 1894 and 1897. Athy and Cill Dara (in Kildare town) opened in the first quarter of the twentieth century. As the century was coming to a close there was a growth of quality courses catering for city folk, often wealthy, who had 'no holes of their own to go to', as a punning Kildare man pronounced!

AND SO TO 2003

The Bartons and the Geraldines may be forgotten as Straffan's Kildare Hotel and Country Club (K-Club) thrives and another luxury hotel and Mark O'Meara-designed golf course emerges at Carton House, Maynooth. The new M9 motorway slices through communities in the south of the county. It and other highways now bypass the main towns.

Kildare town's Racing Academy and Centre for Education (RACE) offers training for farriers and jockeys and boasts a replica main street where European languages may be practised in an authentic setting. There is a maze at Ballynafagh. Kildare County Council has built a new €19m. headquarters at Millennium Park, Naas.

Older Co. Kildare people recall their native county's unspoilt river valleys, canals, bogs and woodlands—quiet backwaters rich in flora and fauna. They appreciate walking routes on the canal towpaths and in forest parks in Donadea, Kilkea and Monasterevin. But they fear for Kildare's easy access to Dublin by road and rail that makes much of the county a developer's dream. Villages have become sprawling dormitory towns. Apart from those counties containing cities, Donegal, Meath and Kildare had the highest growth in new houses in 2001 at 2,722, 2,553 and 2,462 respectively. [14]

Attractive streetscapes and designs are under increasing threat while conservationists attempt to control the proliferation of plastic signs brashly clamouring for attention. Yet the caring people of town and country struggle to protect ancient buildings and historic ruins. They cherish the rich heritage of 'the short grass county' and are vigilant in preserving it for future generations.

8 The ARTS

ARCHITECTURE AND ALLIED WORKS

ARCHITECT NATHANIEL CLEMENTS (1705–1777) of Killadoon, Straffan, designed Newbury Hall, Carbury (c. 1748) and Lodge Park, Straffan (1773). Thomas Ivory (c. 1720–1786) designed a bridge at Carton, Maynooth in 1763. The Scottish architect John MacNeil (1793–1880) designed railway stations at Kildare and Newbridge in 1845. The English architect George E. Street (1824–1881) supervised the restoration of Saint Brigid's Cathedral, Kildare in 1875, while Joseph F. Fuller (1835–1934) worked on the church of Saint Michael and All Angels, Clane in 1883. Architect John Thompson (b. 1917) worked on Saint Dominic's Church, Athy. Features included stained glass and Stations of the Cross by George Campbell (1917–1979). Carnalway, Kilcullen Church of Ireland church has a stained glass window depicting Saint Hubert (1921) by Harry Clarke (1889–1931).

ARTIFACTS

Originally, the Prosperous Crozier was adorned with champleve enamel, a mosaic blue cross and three gemstones. Believed to be of early thirteenth century origin, it was discovered in a bog near Prosperous c. 1840. After restoration work carried out at Queens University, Belfast, it was transferred to Clongowes Wood College museum where it remains.

In 1849, George Petrie (1790–1866), artist, antiquary and musician presented the Kildare (or FitzGerald) Harp to the Fourth Duke of Leinster who closeted it in Kilkea Castle. In an accompanying note, Petrie said it was made for 'the second son of the great house of Kildare' and that he had purchased it from 'a poor woman in Cooke Street', Dublin, who had bought it at an auction. It was later moved to Carton House, Maynooth and is now on display, occasionally, at the National Museum, Collins Barracks, Dublin.

Sir Alfred Chester Beatty (1875–1968) presented a collection of oriental weapons to the Military College, Curragh Camp.

LITERATURE

Kildare's literary tradition goes back to about 1330 when a writer known only as 'Friar Michael of Kildare' wrote sixteen 'Kildare Poems'. In English, French and Latin, their content was satirical, religious and sometimes bawdy. A convention of poets met in Rathangan (see Chapter 9) in 1433. The Co. Kildare born Franciscan, Peter Walsh O.F.M. (c.1614–1688) defended the Royalist cause in the civil wars of 1642–49. After the Restoration of 1660 he published works promoting loyalty to the restored English monarchy. These included *The History and Vindication of the Loyal Formulary of Irish Remonstrance* (1674).

The Leadbeater Papers of Mary Leadbeater (1758–1826) were released in 1862 (see South Kildare, Chapter 6).

For William Napier see Celbridge Abbey, Fine Houses, Chapter 7.

Among the works of the poet Rev. Charles Wolfe (c. 1791–1825) who lived at Blackhall, Clane, was 'On the Burial of Sir John Moore' (1817), described by Lord Byron (1788–1824) as 'the finest Ode in the English language'. He was Wolfe Tone's cousin (see Chapter 6).

The London-born poet Gerard Manley Hopkins (1844–1889) was professor of Greek at the Jesuit University College, Saint Stephen's Green, Dublin. He spent Christmas 1886 in the home of a Miss Cassidy of the Monasterevin brewing family (see The Curse of the Cassidys, Chapter 6) and declared his breaks in the town, where he composed some of his sonnets, as 'one of the props and struts of [his] existence'. From Monasterevin he forwarded at least one sonnet to the British poet/publisher, Robert (Seymore) Bridges (1844–1930), who published Manley's work posthumously (1918). The annual Gerard Manley Hopkins International Summer School began in Monasterevin in 1987.

Teresa Brayton (nee Boylan, c. 1868–1943) of Kilbrook, Cloncurry, wrote the song 'The Old Bog Road'. Allegedly the song celebrates a *bóithrín* close to her home near Kilcock. There are claims that she went to school in the present Newtown Hall, whose drama group takes her name. She was buried in Cloncurry cemetery. She also wrote under the pseudonym T. B. Kilbrook.

Poet William A. Byrne (1872–1933) and novelist and cookery expert Maura Laverty (1907–1966) came from Rathangan.

Stephen Rynne (1901–1980) lived at Downings, Prosperous. He wrote *Green Fields*, an autobiography, in 1938, *All Ireland,* a travel book, in 1956 and a biography, *Canon John Hayes* (Founder of Muintir na Tíre). His wife, Alice Curtayne (1901–1991) wrote six books, among them *Irish Saints for Boys and Girls* and biographies of Patrick Sarsfield, Saint Catherine of Siena and Francis Ledwidge.

Not wishing her hunting and social friends to know she was writing, Molly Keane (née Mary Nesta Skrine (1904–1996)) took her pseudonym M.J. Farrell from a pub sign in Co. Tipperary, where she lived for some time. Biographies give her place of birth as Co. Kildare, and in some cases, Connelmore. This may be Conall Mór, the Irish for Great Connell, near Newbridge but, remarkably, biographical details are not precise. She began writing at seventeen years of age. Her many novels included *The Rising Tide* (1937) and *Loving Without Tears* (1951). She gave up writing for a long period before her *Good Behaviour* (1981) was shortlisted for the Booker prize and was televised in 1983. *Loving and Giving* (1988) was her last novel. She wrote three plays. Her Antrim-born mother Agnes Nesta Skrine wrote under the name Moira O'Neill.

Although born in India in 1911, the distinguished maritime and military historian and author John Evan de Courcy Ireland was the son of an army major serving in the Curragh.

Long-time Newbridge resident Desmond Egan (1936–) is a major international award-winning poet. His work includes sixteen collections of poems, a collection of prose, *The Death of a Metaphor* (1990 and 1991), and two translations of Greek plays. Sixteen of his books are in translation and he has been the subject of two critical studies and two video documentaries on his life and work. Eminent tributes to his work include ' . . . the poet of our age' and 'what James Joyce did for Dublin and W.B. Yeats did for Sligo, Egan has done for the Irish midlands'. *Midland* (1972), *Athlone?* (1980), *Poems for Peace* (1986) and *Famine* (1997) are among his distinguished works.

Sculptor, poet and playwright James McKenna (1933–2000) was a Macaulay Fellowship recipient who lived and worked in Newbridge from 1988 until his death. His large figures in wood, limestone and granite are to be seen in a number of institutions and residences at home and abroad. He wrote *The Scatterin'* (1960), a musical play, and a drama *At Bantry* (1967). The gallery in Newbridge Riverside Arts Centre is named in his honour.

Aidan Higgins (1927–) of Celbridge is a novelist and short story writer. His work is Baroque in style and includes *Langrishe, Go Down* (1966) a novel of a house in decline, *Balcony of Europe* (1972) and a collection *Asylum* (earlier *Felo de Se* (1960)).

Con Costello, Naas, contributed a weekly column on local history to the *Leinster Leader*. His books include *Botany Bay* (Dublin and Cork, 1987) and *A Most Delightful Station* (Cork, 1996).

Michael Kavanagh, Kildare County Librarian has compiled a *Bibliography of the History of Co. Kildare in Printed Books* (Naas, 1976) and the library's local history section's Mario Corrigan (1964–) has written on the 1798 Rebellion in a number of publications and in his book *All That Delirium of the Brave–Kildare in 1798* (Naas, 1997).

Padraic O'Farrell (1932–), the author of this *History of County Kildare* was born in Staplestown, Donadea. He has written scripts for leading Irish performers, forty books on Irish life and lore including five in a Gill & Macmillan series featuring the theme: *Irish Saints, Irish Surnames, Ancient Irish Legends* and *Irish Fairy Tales*. His book *The Burning of Brinsley MacNamara* (Dublin, 1990) examines the events that surrounded the publication of Brinsley MacNamara's *succes de scandale, The Valley of the Squinting Windows*. His other works include short biographies of Sean MacEoin and Ernie O'Malley, *Who's Who in the Irish War of Independence and Civil War 1916–23* (Dublin, 1997) a novel on Michael Collins *Rebel Heart* (Dublin and Dingle, 1990/1996), two historical plays and a musical.

Leland Bardwell (1928–) was born in India of Irish parents but grew up in Leixlip. She was a founder member of the Irish Writers' Co-op and has written plays and poems, a short story collection and five novels. *Mother to a Stranger* (Belfast, 2002) is her latest.

MUSIC

Nás na Ríogh Singers had successes performing a range of classical choral works at prestigious events. Marie Slowey of Newbridge was a conductor of note and her husband, Con Sullivan, directed musicals throughout the country.

Jimmy Dunny from Newbridge was one of the first dance bands in Ireland to feature the Hammond organ. By the time the band stopped performing in the 1990s it had become the country's longest performing dance band. In ceilí music, the Gallowglass band of Naas was one of the oldest.

Prosperous could claim to have begun the ballad boom of the 1960s. Christy Moore and Donal Lunny of Newbridge began their singing career there and 'Prosperous' was the name of an early album. As Luka Bloom, Moore's brother Andy also became a successful solo artist. Fionnuala Sherry from Kildare won the Eurovision Song Contest for Norway in 1995. The voice of Athy's Jack L has captured the popular imagination at the start of the twenty-first century.

PAINTING

The English painter Francis Wheatley (1747–1801) painted the *Salmon Weir* at Leixlip in 1780. William Ashford (1746–1824) painted *Leixlip Castle* in 1794 and *The Cascade at Carton* in 1800. Francis Danby (1793–1861) painted *Disappointed Love* (Athy Civic Buildings 1822). Michael Angelo Hayes (1820–1877) painted five plates under the title *The Race for the Punchestown Cup* in 1854.

Although born in Dublin, Francis Bacon (1909–1992) lived for some time in Cannycourt, near Kilcullen. His family also lived in Straffan House. Francis made his name with his 1945 work *Three figures at the Base of a Crucifixion*.

SCULPTURE

A number of ancient stoneworks have been recorded throughout this book. Others include the Bermingham tomb at Dunfierth (c. 1548) and the Aylmer monument at Saint Peter's Church, Donadea (c. 1634).

Mary Redmond (1790–1861) from Ardclough sculpted the Father Matthew statue in Dublin and a bust of the British Prime Minister William E. Gladstone (1775–1802). Imogen Stuart (née Werner 1927–) sculpted the Stations of the Cross in the Curragh Camp Church in 1957.

Specialising in wood sculpture, Father Henry Flanagan taught at the Dominican College, Newbridge up to his death in 1992. The college church contains his Stations of the Cross, *Crucifixion Group* and *Madonna and Child*. Other Newbridge schools feature his work.

Bridget Rynne (Bríd Ní Rinn), daughter of Stephen and Alice (see Literature, above) sculpted a crucifix for Saint Dominic's Church, Athy.

THEATRE AND TELEVISION

Frank Carney's (1902–1977) play *The Righteous Are Bold* (1946) is, allegedly, based on a satanic possession of a priest's housekeeper in Allen. The village of Allen has a strong amateur drama tradition.

Kildare Drama Festival was founded in 1958 under the auspices of Muintir na Tíre (People of the Country). The Moat Club, Naas won the All-Ireland Amateur Drama Finals in 1974, 1979 and 2000.

Micheál Mac Liammoir (1899–1978) gave his first performance of the celebrated one-man show *The Importance of Being Oscar* in the Gaelic Hall, Curragh Camp.

Actor Tom Hickey is a native of Naas. He won his place on the county Gaelic football team before embarking on a distinguished acting career on stage, in television and in films. He collaborated successfully with playwright Tom MacIntyre on a number of occasions.

Castledermot-born John McKenna (1952–) is a television producer, biographer and novelist who now lives in Athy. His published works include *The Fallen and Other Stories* (1993), *Clare* (1994) and a biography of Ernest Shackleton (2002). He has worked with Mend & Makedo Theatre Company for whom he wrote dramatic works including *Sergeant Pepper*, *The Unclouded Days* and *Who by Fire*.

Crooked House Theatre Company Ltd. originated in Newbridge in 1994.

Maynooth's Pope John Paul II and Russell libraries are magnificent repositories. Kildare County Library is situated in the fine modern Riverside Arts Complex at Newbridge. It has branches at Athy, Ballitore, Celbridge, Kilcock, Leixlip, Maynooth and Naas. All three libraries and their staffs have contributed enormously to research for the writing of this book.

A MISCELLANY Of PLACES
And PEOPLE, ODDMENTS
And ODDITIES,
HAPPENINGS And
HOUSES, ARTS And
ARTISTS

9

ALLEN

(ALMHAN, FORMERLY ALMÚ.** White material [in the walls of Fionn Mac Cumhaill's palace]) Some people believe that a seven-foot skeleton discovered at Allen was that of Fionn, who had his headquarters on the Hill of Allen.

The hill is an important mythological site, being the home of the Sidh of Nuada, the greatest of the Celtic gods. He was twice king of the Tuatha Dé Danaan and son of the mother of the god, Zeus. Nuadha's sword is mentioned in Arthurian legend. At the battle of Allen (see Chapter 4) Fergal Mac Máile Dúin was beheaded. His head was washed and placed on a spear on which the battle goddess Badb perched in the form of a raven. Sir Gerald Aylmer of Donadea Castle built the tower on a burial mound at the peak. A tunnel is thought to connect it with his castle at Donadea. It is said that if a human being crossed a certain stile between the two locations at the stroke of midnight, he would be transfixed.

ARDCLOUGH

(Árd Clocha/Height of stones) It had a limestone quarry and its stony men were once noted for fist-fighting at football matches, especially when pitted against Carbury (below, and see Sculpture, Chapter 8).

ARDRASS

(Árd Ras/Wooded height) Saint Patrick's Chapel is a restored fifteenth century stone-roofed structure. Ireland has many wells and 'beds' of the saint and one of each stands here.

ARDSCULL

(Árd Scoil/Height of the [hedge] school) Its motte or perhaps pre-historic burial mound was later a Cromwellian fortification.

ATHY

(Ath Aé/The ford of Aé) Mullagh-Reelan, now a mound near Kilkea Castle, was an ancient royal palace, as was Maistiu, now known as the Rath of Mullamast,

The Earl of Kildare built White's Castle (c. 1500) to defend the strategic Barrow river crossing. Woodstock Castle near the town became a stronghold of Richard de St Michael and Owen Roe O'Neill occupied it during the War of the Confederacy.

The ruins of Ballyadams Castle remain four miles south of Athy. Sir John Bowen, Parliamentary Provost Marshal of Leinster and Meath, was holding it on lease during the Tudor plantation. His cruelty earned him the nickname Seán an Phíce (John of the Pike) He defied the call of Royalist General Cavendish (see Chapter 4) to surrender by saying 'I will cover that part, or any other your Lordship shoots at by hanging there my daughters tied in chairs'.

Little remains of Rheban Castle, a former stronghold of Richard de Saint Michael. Once, remains of a hand clasping money were discovered in the masonry, as if its owner was severely punished for stealing. The finder respectfully allowed the hand to remain where it was–after removing the money!

The Earl of Castlehaven and Derby, James Touchet (Lord Audley. d. 1631) was General of Thomas Preston's Leinster Horse (see More Rebellion, Chapter 5). The Irish Earldom had been restored to Touchet after he had testified against his father who had been tried and executed for rape, homosexuality and sodomy amid allegations of being 'seduced by the Instigation of the Devil, and of 'Wickedly, Devilishly [and] Feloniously commit[ting] that Detestable Abominable Sin.' The trial produced evidence of an unpleasant orgy involving the man's wife, a sailor and an Irishman. It remained a legal precedent in homosexual cases for 200 years. Suspected Roman Catholic sympathies of the accused led the Attorney General to remark 'when once a Man indulges his Lust, and Prevaricates with his Religion, as my Lord Audley has done, by being a Protestant in the Morning, and a Papist in the Afternoon, no wonder if he commits the most abominable Impieties.'

BALLITORE

(Béal Atha an Tuair/Mouth of the ford of the bleach green) Mary Shackleton-Leadbeater became interested in writing and corresponded with Maria Edgeworth (1767–1849) and with the Suffolk poet George Crabbe (1754–1832). She kept an *Annals of Ballitore* for fifty years. They represent an important account of village life; a sort of 'Under Milk Wood' for Co. Kildare country life. Mary's husband, William (1763–1827), was of Huguenot parents who fled France due to the revocation of the Edict of Nantes. He lived with the Shackletons from the age of fourteen. He married Mary in 1791 and taught French in Ballitore school. Mary Leadbeater described an incident that was not in keeping with Quaker pacifism:

> *Young boys are the same whatever the age and the school had its fair share of jokers. In one incident the pupils, anxious at the approach of summer, took possession of the school and locked out the staff including the Master, Abraham!*

In those early times there was a lad at school, Henry Graham by name. He was in the army, and received pay; his manners and air were military. A 'barring-out' took place, and Abraham Shackleton, after having tried other methods in vain, forced the door with a sledgehammer. While this was being done, the garrison strove to capitulate. They asked for 'a week's play'. 'No'. 'An evening's play'. 'No'. 'Pardon for their fault'. 'No'. Graham snapped a pistol, which missed fire. The offenders were led to punishment. Those who expressed sorrow for what they had done escaped the dreaded whipping. Graham would not, and was whipped. He was then asked was he sorry now? 'No'. He was whipped again. 'Was he sorry?' 'Yes; he was sorry that the pistol had missed fire!'

Cardinal Paul Cullen (1803–1878) of Prospect received his early education in the Shackleton Quaker school. He is credited with drafting the dogma on papal infallibility.

BALLYMORE EUSTACE

(Baile Mór Eustace/Large homestead of Eustace). Since the late fourteenth century the FitzEustace line has been connected with Calverstown, Castlemartin, Clongowes Wood and Harristown, and with this town bearing the name. There, they were hereditary constables of the Archbishop of Dublin's manor house. Canadian-born Florence Nightingale Graham (1878–1966), better known as the beautician and businesswoman Elizabeth Arden, owned Barretstown Castle. It later became the first European model of Oscar winner Paul Newman's (1925–) American Hole-in-the-Wall Gang Camp. Barretstown Gang Camp aims at giving seriously ill European children a chance to rediscover their childhood.

BALLYNAFAGH

(Baile na Faiche/Homestead of the green) Wintering fowl come to the reservoir of the Grand Canal, near Prosperous. There is also a 'Millennium Maze' in the area.

BETAGHSTOWN

A biateach (Bi Teach/House of food) was a house of hospitality, kept by Irish chieftains. Monks or laymen received land and stock to enable them to run these households and the property was known as a bailebeteach. The Anglicisation to Betaghstown is obvious.

CARAGH

(Corrach/Swamp) Caragh Birds' Nest was the name of an orphanage near the Cock bridge. In 1892 Rev Samuel Cotton and his wife were charged with maltreatment of their charges there. At the end of the nineteenth century there occurred the 'Clongorey Evictions' in the area and throughout Dereens and Clongorey, three miles south west.

CARBURY

(Cairbre. From cairbreach, meaning rocky or ridged or perhaps Cairbre, son of Niall of the Nine Hostages) One of the most popular pattern days in Co. Kildare was held at 'The Sweep of Carbury'. Carbury Castle is the ruin of a Jacobean manor house beside a bailey (once with motte). De Berminghams were the original owners (see Johnstownbridge, below). From the sixteenth century, Colleys and later Wellesleys, ancestors of the Arthur Wellesley, First Duke of Wellington (1769–1852) were occupants.

CASTLEDERMOT

(Díseart Díarmuid/Dermot's hermitage). Crutched Friars and Franciscans had priories in Castledermot, which has a round tower and two high crosses (see Chapter 3). An early sixteenth century Tallon tomb bears a cross with female and male cadavers.

CELBRIDGE

(Cill Droichead/Church of the bridge) A broken mirror in Castletown House is offered as evidence of a struggle that took place between Speaker Conolly and the Devil. All day long a mysterious rider outjumped Conolly in the chase. Gallant towards this superior horseman, Conolly invited him back to dinner. While playing cards afterwards, Conolly dropped one and noticed the stranger had a cloven foot. A struggle ensued but the Devil was uncontrollable. The local curate was called and after throwing the mirror at the holy man praying before him, 'Old Nick' disappeared up the chimney in a puff of smoke. Folklorists tell a similar tale about 'Hellfire Clubs' in Counties Dublin and Wexford, however.

During the eighteenth century, the ladies of Castletown and Carton, the Lennox sisters, dominated. The Leinster Papers reveal bouts of boredom suffered by Lady Amelia Lennox (1730–1814) at Carton. She was the First Duchess of Leinster and wife of James Edward FitzGerald, Twentieth Earl of Kildare and First Duke of Leinster. They were married in 1747. A letter written eight years later says 'My new post-chaise is vastly pretty ... I have a silver loo party ... almost every night and loose all my money [five or six guineas], but what can I do? Cards are a necessary evil.'

CLANE

(Claonadh/Slanted [ford] or Cluain Ath/Meadow of the Ford) 'A Clane woman should marry a Prosperous man,' they say in this historic town. There, an early Ulster poet and druid called Áthairne the Important visited the King of Leinster, Mesgora Mac Da Thó, and attempted to invoke the laws of hospitality whereby a guest could demand a host's wife. Mesgora refused, because he loved his beautiful spouse, Buan. Áthairne then urged the Ulster king, Conchobar Mac Nessa, to declare war on the Leinster king which he did and attacked Clane. Áthairne killed Mesgora at the ford and on discovering her husband's body his wife Buan died beside him. She was buried at Úaig Búana, believed to be beneath a mound at nearby Mainham.

Some biographers of James Joyce say that he hired a Clane hackney-car to bring him from Clongowes Wood College to Sallins railway station. In his retirement, the tenor Josef Locke drank in Jones's public house in Clane.

CLONGOWES WOOD

(Coill Chlúana Gabhann/The wood of the smith's meadow. See Modern) 'Gowes' boys were mostly sons of wealthy people. A pernicious nickname for domestic servants working in the college was 'slavies'. The college once competed in sports against the Dominican College, Newbridge and the Military College's Cadet School on the Curragh. The trophy was 'The Golden Sword'. James Joyce believed the Jesuits in Clongowes Wood and Belvedere College taught him 'how to order and to judge'. He knew of the phantom black dog with 'eyes as big as carriage lamps' that roamed the college's corridors and of the ghost in blood-stained military uniform. Two Wogan Browne girls witnessed it and knew their brother was dead. They held a wake and were proved right. Marshal Wogan Browne was killed in Prague at the time they saw the apparition.

CURRAGH

(An Currach sometimes Currach Life/The racecourse or marsh [of the Liffey].) Towards the end of the Boer War (c. 1901), two lines of regimental officers kicked a homosexual paedophile, Captain Richard Gorges out of his South African station for interfering with a young drummer boy. His distinguished family had the affair hushed up and so Gorges was posted to the Curragh as a musketry instructor. Gorges befriended Frank Shackleton, the Dublin Herald allegedly involved in the theft of the Irish 'Crown Jewels' (see Maynooth College, Chapter 7).

DONADEA

(Domhnach Déagh. Domhnach is a derivative of the Latin *dominicum*, meaning church. So Dea's [or God's] church) Donadea Castle was an

Aylmer seat (see Personalities, Chapter 6), the latest designed by Richard Morrisson. A church alongside contained a Renaissance canopied tomb. A table-tennis club played in its west tower during 'The Emergency' and it had its ghosts—a 'White Woman' and a headless horseman driving phantom steeds and a carriage along its splendid Lime Avenue. A local labourer almost lost his hand while sawing timber for a charcoal manufacturer's pyre (see Industry, Chapter 7). His Italian employer remarked 'Hands no make good charcoal!'

FIRMOUNT

Thomas Dease (1558–1652) was a professor at Sorbonne, Paris before becoming Bishop of Meath (1621–52). Later in that century, his nephew, Oliver, was Vicar General of the diocese. Saint Oliver Plunkett (1625–1681) was also a relative. A later Oliver Dease was a surgeon who resided at Stafford Street, now Wolfe Tone Street, Dublin and served in the British Navy, probably under a false name. His brother, Richard, lived at Firmount House, near Clane, from 1794 until his death in 1838. He used his influence with Hugh Ware (see Personalities, Chapter 6) to prevent the United Irishmen from burning Firmount House during the 1798 rebellion. Oliver and his wife Anne were there when their daughter, Ellen (1820–1899) was born. After an education in France, Ellen returned to Dublin and joined the Institute of the Blessed Virgin Mary, better known as the Loreto nuns, in Rathfarnham. They later dropped one 't' in Dublin but retained it in Canada. After her profession in 1847 as Sister Mary Teresa, Ellen and four other nuns founded the Loretto order in Toronto and went on to establish thirteen more branches in North America.

Throughout the nineteenth century, tuberculosis became a major cause of death in Ireland. Epidemics continued into the twentieth century and it became known as the 'Irish Disease'. In 1908, the Tuberculosis Prevention (Ireland) Act authorized county councils to provide sanatoria. One of these was at Firmount House.

During World War One, repatriated British soldiers who had been wounded were returning from the Western Front in such numbers that the Curragh Military Hospital authorities had to seek extra accommodation. In June 1917, they placed forty beds in Firmount and attended to almost 400 patients there within a year.

Doctor Noël Browne (1915–1997), as Minister for Health in the first Inter-Party Government (1948–51) launched a major campaign to eradicate tuberculosis and Firmount reverted to its former function until 1961 under the name Saint Conleth's Sanatorium.

In 1964 the Department of Defence purchased Firmount House from Kildare County Council and in 1966 it became Dublin County Control, Kildare County Control and also Number Seven Regional Control for Civil Defence.

FURNESS

There are claims that the name, often spelt Furnish, Furnance or Furnace, recalls Anglo-Norman iron-smelting furnaces. Furness House may have been designed by Francis Bindon in 1731. The Nevilles were early occupants and the gallaun of Forenaughts is close by.

GRANGE HILL

Close to the Hill of Allen there is a lesser slope, called the Hill of Grange. A small house clinging to its side was the home of Moll Anthony. Most practitioners in the art of curing confined their cases to ailments of humans but ' . . . the rale old Moll Anthony of the Red Hills . . .' seems to have also had a veterinary degree. Moreover, she did not always attend at the farms of the sick beasts; once the animal's owner came to Moll, the beast was cured at the moment of consultation!

One of the many stories told about Moll is about how a boy once met a funeral and, as was the custom, turned to walk some of the way behind the coffin, even helping to carry it. When the funeral came back to the boy's own gate the pallbearers left down the coffin. The boy ran in to tell his mother and when they both came back out the coffin was still there but the mourners were gone. The lid was unscrewed and a young girl stepped from within. She lived with the family, taking the mother's name, Mary. When she and the boy, James, grew up, they married.

One day the young wife asked James to bring her with him to the fair in Castledermot. During the day an old farmer remarked to James that his bride was 'the spit' of his own daughter, buried many years before. The old farmer's wife agreed and quoted the date of their daughter's death. It coincided with the day James saw the girl step from the coffin. Mary even admitted it, for as the old farmer's wife ordered her to pull down the top of her dress she said, 'It's all right, mother; the raspberry mark is still on my shoulder'. Those who held Moll Anthony to be in league with the 'good people', believed her to have been that girl, Mary (Moll).

GREAT CONNELL

There is no trace of the Augustinian priory founded in 1202, but an effigy of a prior who was Master of the Rolls, Walter Wellesley (d.c. 1539), and panels from his tomb remain.

HALVERSTOWN

William Makepeace Thackeray (1811–1863) once spent a while on the farm of a Purcell family and wrote about their way of life. Tradition has it that an inn called 'Ten of the Hundred' there got its name because all but ten of every hundred guests were robbed or killed.

JOHNSTOWN

The Sixth Earl of Mayo was assassinated in 1872 when Governor of India. Local lore proclaims that his body was transported home in a hogshead of rum for interment in Johnstown, thus earning him the soubriquet 'The Pickled Earl'.

JOHNSTOWNBRIDGE

One of Ireland's few explosives factory is in Cloonagh, close to this village at the Co. Meath border. Some believe that the oddly named Fear English river and bridge recall a massacre of the Carbury Berminghams by the O'Ruaircs of Breffny.

KILCOCK

(Cill Chóca/Saint Coca's Church. See Brigid, Christianity).

> *The town of Naas is a terrible place*
> *Kilcock is just as bad*
> *But of all the places I've ever been*
> *Well * * * * you, Kinnegad.*

What American influence brought the town Ireland's first mail order business, 'Cotts of Kilcock', and the first chewing gum factory?

KILCULLEN

(Cill Chuillinn/The Church [on] the steep incline) A large black dog was said to haunt Castlemartin House (see Personalities, Chapter 6 and Fine Houses, Chapter 7). The present owner is Sir A.J. O'Reilly. Old Kilcullen has the remains of a round tower and of a Romanesque church and crosses (see Chapter 6).

KILDARE

(Cill Daire/The Church of the Oak) Bishop Ralph of Bristol (see Chapter 3) probably initiated the construction of Saint Brigid's Cathedral (c. 1229). Restoration took place in 1875. A 33-metre-high round tower has a Romanesque door and modern parapet. The alleged site of Saint Brigid's fire is close by. Kildare's artillery barracks was the first constructed for the army by the new state after the War of Independence, but has now been vacated.

KILKEA

(Cill Chathaigh/Cathach's church) The medieval castle reconstructed in 1849 was associated with the 'Wizard' (Eleventh) Earl of Kildare (see The Geraldines Again, Chapter 5). It was later the seat of the Dukes of

Leinster. A carving high on its wall receives little mention, but when it does it is said to represent an animal attacking a saint, i.e. temptation. Close examination reveals the likelihood that it suggests bestiality.

While Europe was smarting at the outbreak of the Great War, Ernest Shackleton (1874–1922) of Kilkea Castle was setting off for the Antarctic in HMS *Endurance*. He had already accompanied Robert Falcon Scott (1868–1912) in his 1901–04 expedition that discovered King Edward VII Land. He also led a 1909 expedition that reached a spot 161 kilometres short of the South Pole. For this, he was knighted. Pack ice thwarted his progress in 1914 and he had to be rescued after covering 3,200 kilometres by various methods. He was to try again in 1921 but died in South Georgia on 5 January 1922.

Ernest's brother Frank was Dublin Herald and was accused of involvement in the 1907 theft of the Irish Crown Jewels, often regarded as a Loyalist intrigue designed to discredit the Viceroy, Lord Aberdeen who supported Home Rule (see Maynooth College, Chapter 7).

KILL

(An Chill/The Church) From the seventh to the twelfth century Leinster kings were buried in Kill.

KILLASHEE

(Cill Ausaile or Cell Auxili/Church of [Bishop] Auxilius) Auxilius was a missionary bishop who settled close to Royal Naas in the fifth century. To be near the seat of Leinster power, probably!

Before becoming a hotel, the manor house was a boarding school, and bold Co. Kildare children were threatened by strict parents with 'I'll send you to Killashee'.

KILMEAGUE

(Cill Maodhóg/[Saint] Maodhóg's church)

For my poor heart is breakin'
Since Kilmeague I have forsaken
And it's back there I'll be makin'
For this England I don't care.
I would sooner turf be footin'
While my father would be cuttin'
Or the cottage door be shuttin'
In my home in old Kildare.

When Daniel O'Connell (1775–1847) and the Irish MPs held the balance of power in the House of Commons and supported the Whig government of 1832–41, there was violent agitation against paying tithes and crime was rampant. Protestant landlords became fearful and began protecting themselves. A Reverend Preston founded Kilmeague village for that purpose.

KILTEEL

(Cill tSíle/Síle's church). In the local cemetery, rare figure-sculptures are included in reconstructed remains of a Romanesque church close to a tower house. They represent Adam, Eve, Samson, David and unidentified athletes.

KNOCKAULIN

(Cnoc Álainn/Beautiful hill) is believed to be Dún Áilinne, the early seat of Leinster's kings because of embanked roadways leading to a significant rampart and ditch mark.

LEIXLIP

(Léim an Bradáin/Salmon Leap. Danish *Lax-hlaup*) In the fifteenth century, Henry VII (1457–1509) made Leixlip a Crown possession. The town's twelfth century castle is modernised. The FitzGerald Earls of

Kildare, Whites and Conollys owned it up to 1914. A complete refurbishment took place in the eighteenth century. Lord Decies carried out further alterations in 1914. Messrs. William Kavanagh and Desmond Guinness were later owners (see Good for You, Chapter 7). The town's Church of Ireland church has a medieval tower.

MAYNOOTH

(Maigh Nuadh/Nuada's Plain.) (See Allen, above) The town's celebrated college has an oratory that, allegedly, was converted after a student committed suicide in his room there and others attempted to do so. The hair of a priest who kept a vigil in it after the incident turned white overnight. A resolution of the college trustees dated 23 October 1860 suggested 'That the President be authorised to convert room No. 2 on the top corridor of Rhetoric House into an oratory of Saint Joseph . . .'

MONASTEREVIN

(Mainistir Eimhín/[Saint] Eimhín's monastery). Saint Eimhín hailed from Cashel and was the legendary son of Eoghan Mór (Big John), who fathered the Munster Eoghanachta. During solemn trials, the tribe swore oaths upon the saint's bell. A clanger was dropped if a false promise was made upon it, because the bell leaped in the air, and could well fall on the perpetrator! Eimhín brought the bell to Monasterevin. Particularly perturbed by a sixth-century perjurer one day, it hopped so high that it dropped into the River Figile and was never found.

An eighteen-day siege of a house in Monasterevin brought world media attention. On 7 November 1975, Marion Coyle and Eddie Gallagher surrendered to Gardai and released the Dutch industrialist Doctor Tiede Herrema whom they had kidnapped.

MOONE

(Maoin/Gift or Property) Entrance pillars to Belan House, the former elegant home of the Earls of Aldborough complement numerous important Christian archaeological features (see Chapter 3).

Squire Yeates of Moone Abbey was a 1798 informer who, when threatened with execution by the rebels, asked to be buried within sight of his home. In 1945, excavators discovered a rusty pike-head impaled in a male skull nearby. Yeates?

MOYVALLEY

(Mágh Bhealaigh/The plain of the pass.) Here once stood the only Co. Kildare hotel on the Royal Canal. A newspaper report described a fracas taking place in a field nearby. Roisterers had collected around a stolen barrel of porter, the contents of which they were enjoying. They were on an excursion from Dublin and were members of a Temperance Society! Later, there was a spa on the site and later still, a catering complex which grew from a roadside caravan whose proprietor, in pre-politically correct times, advertised for a female assistant. He said she needed to be hard-working and an early riser and 'not too fat, because there is not much room in the place'.

MULLAMAST

Oral tradition records that a man called Nolan saw the Rath of Mullamast illuminated one night, entered it and beheld a group of slumbering warriors. He was withdrawing a particularly attractive sword from a scabbard and awoke its owner who asked 'Has the time come?' The terrified Nolan slapped back the weapon into its scabbard, whereupon the warrior fell back asleep (see Wizards and Sceptres, Chapter 5).

Mullamast was the setting for another dark episode, on New Year's Day 1577. *The Annals of the Four Masters* records:

> *The English of Leinster and Meath, upon that part of the people of Offaly and Leix [Laois] that remained in confederacy with them and under their protection committed*

a horrible and abominable act of treachery. It was effected thus: they were all summoned to show themselves with the greatest number they could be able to bring with them at the great Rath of Mullach Maistean; and on their arrival at that place they were surrounded on every side by four lines of soldiers and cavalry who proceeded to slaughter them without mercy so that not a single individual escaped by flight or force.

A Captain Francis Cosby with reinforcements from Kildare town and from Monasterevin perpetrated the atrocity, sources say. Some of the Seven Septs of Laois were victims and their Chiefs were slaughtered in a hollow within the Rath the 'Blood Hole'. Just one escaped. He was an O'More and he lived to perpetuate the Laois sept. Locals believed that widows of the murdered chiefs cursed Cosby and for seven generations the head of a Cosby family never lived to see his eldest son come of age. Stories about ghosts of the massacred frequenting the Rath were common for years. Richard D'Alton Williams (1822–1862) reinforced the belief:

> *O'er the Rath of Mullaghmast,*
> *On the solemn midnight blast*
> *What bleeding spectres passed?*
> *With their gashed breasts bare?*
> *Hast thou heard the fitful wail*
> *That o'erloads the sullen gale*
> *When the waning moon shines pale*
> *O'er the crust ground there?*

NAAS

(Nás na Ríogh/Naas of the Kings) Some folklorists tell that Lugh Lamhfada's wife was called Naas and that she was buried on the site of the present town. The word also suggests a fair or place of assembly. Because it was the main residence of Leinster's kings up to 908, 'Naas of the Kings' emerged. In 1671, King Charles II granted a new charter, incorporating the town 'by name of Sovereign, Portreeves, Burgesses and Commons, and to have liberties belonging to any free borough. It was not taken out until eighteen years later, when Edmond Sherlock became Town Clerk on a salary of £12/0/0 per annum. In the meantime the authorities made a major decision: 'Ye May-pole to be fortwith pulled down and made a lader [sic] of for ye use of ye towne'.

From 1956 to 1998 the Army Apprentice School was located in Devoy Barracks, Naas. The barracks was formerly a depot of the Royal Dublin Fusiliers.

NEWBRIDGE

(Droichead Nua) 'All to one side like the town of Newbridge' was a Co. Kildare saying when the drab wall of the old cavalry barracks built in 1816 formed one side of its main street. In that barracks, the leader of the 'Charge of the Light Brigade' at Balaclava (25 October 1854) in the Crimea served. He was James T. Brudenell, Seventh Earl of Cardigan (1797–1868) after whom the popular knitted garment is called. The celebrated crystalographer, Dame Kathleen Lonsdale (née Yardley 1903–71) was born in the town. She became Professor of Chemistry at University College, London and in 1945 became the first female Fellow of the Royal Society (see Chapter 8).

NURNEY

(An Urnaí/The oratory) At the northern and southern extremities of Co. Kildare are places called Nurney.

OUGHTERARD

(Uachtar Árd/Upper height) A 10-metre-high round tower has an unusual entrance with inclined supports. William, Lord Ponsonby, and the Earl of Clonmell occupied it.

POLLARDSTOWN

'A Snail's Progress' was the newspaper headline announcing the delay in motorway planning permission due to a rare specimen of snail in Pollardstown Fen, an area of considerable ecological importance.

PROSPEROUS

(An English name bestowed by Robert Brook in 1776 but the Irish name is An Chorrchoill, normally 'wood of the weir' but most likely 'odd' or 'projecting wood') There are strong suggestions that a coffin-maker called Matthew Tone who was Wolfe Tone's brother, lived at Mapletoft Hall, later a presbytery (see Chapter 6).

PUNCHESTOWN

When Punchestown Long Stone fell in 1931, it measured 7 metres in length. It weighed 9.15 tonnes and marked a stone cist. The Woolpack Road near Punchestown was part of a medieval highway from Dublin through Rathcoole and Kilteel. It continued on through Kilcullen, Athgarvan and Athy, on its way to Kilkenny. Its name may have derived from its usefulness in bringing wool from Wicklow and Curragh sheep to the cities.

RATHANGAN

(Ráth Iomghán/Fort of Iomghán) has a dramatic range of late Georgian and Victorian architecture including a stone bridge of 1784. The fort of the name (officially classed as a 'ringfort' by the Ordnance Survey) stands outside the town. Offaly's pride, Margaret O'Carroll 'The Bountiful' and the 'best woman of her time in Ireland' gave one of her celebrated lavish feasts in Rathangan in 1433. Almost 2,700 poets, gamesters and poor men attended.

In 2001, Brian Dowling, a young gay man from Rathangan, became a television celebrity after being voted the most popular member of Channel 4's 'Big Brother' household.

RATHCOFFEY

(Ráth Cobhthaigh/[O]Coffey's Fort. Some suggest fort of victory (cobhthach)) Sir Charles 'Chevalier' Wogan (c. 1698–1754) was a Jacobite mercenary who fought at Preston in 1715 during the Stuart rebellion. He became a baronet and, at the instigation of Pope Innocent XIII, a Roman senator.

ROBERTSTOWN

(See Canals, Chapter 7) A Co. Kildare Saint Stephen's Day 'Wren boy' rhyme went, in part:

> *I whooshed her up and I whooshed her down*
> *And I whooshed her into Robertstown*
> *I dipped her head in a barrel of beer*
> *And I wish you all a Happy New Year.*

SALLINS

(Saileán/Willow-bed) During the 1798 rebellion, an officer and twenty men guarded Sallins canal bridge and there was still a 'Soldiers' Island' nearby when a railway bridge on the Naas branch held a pillbox and girder defences during World War Two.

STAPLESTOWN

(Baile an tSéipéil/Town of the chapel) The life of a schoolmaster in Staplestown is told in *Tell Me, Sean O'Farrell* (Dublin & Cork 1986) written by the author of this history.

STRAFFAN

(An Sruthán/The small stream) Lodge Park, a late eighteenth century residence of a banker that passed on to the Guinness family, is now a steam museum.

Also in the eighteenth century, John Joseph Henry married Lady Emily FitzGerald, daughter of the Duke of Leinster. He was one of the wealthiest men of his time, yet his spendthrift ways forced him to sell Straffan House. Members of the family emigrated and became prominent in public life in Maryland, USA. A later resident, Hugh Barton, was a Bordeaux wine merchant. He used Straffan as an escape from a French purge of 1793–94 when foreign businessmen were cast into prison. He arranged for a partner, Daniel Guestier, to continue the business that has survived to this day. The B & G label is highly regarded by even the most fastidious palates. Ronald Barton was the latest representative of the Straffan Family at the Bordeaux concern. He served with the British and Free French forces during World War Two. The Germans occupied Chateau Leoville Barton. When informed that the establishment was Irish, they looted no cellars and damaged no property, though perhaps they did call for the bottle of Paddy whiskey hidden behind the Cuvée Thomas Barton!

Of the Glendalough branch of the family, Robert Barton was the longest surviving signatory of the Anglo-Irish Treaty when he died in 1975. Straffan House is now the Kildare Hotel and Country Club (K Club) and its golf course was chosen as the venue for the 2005 Ryder Cup competition.

TAGHADOE

(Teach Túa/Saint Tua's House). Locals call it 'Taptoo' and the 19-metre-high round tower marking the site of the saint's monastery may have been unfinished. He was also called 'Ultan the Silent'.

TIMAHOE

(Tigh Mochuada/Mochua's House) Quaker ancestors of the former President of the United States Richard Nixon (1913–1994) were buried in Timahoe graveyard. As president, Nixon visited Timahoe in October 1970.

TIMOLIN

(Tigh Mólin/[Saint] Moling's House) An old mill here is used as a pewter manufacturing workshop (see Chapter 3).

Appendix

1. COUNTY KILDARE MEMBERS OF PARLIAMENT (MPS)

R. Archbold, R. Archdall, W. Bayley, Lieutenant Colonel Overington Blunden, Rt Hon. D. Browne. R.S. Bourke, R. Burke, Hon. C.H. Butler, P.S. Butler, J.L. Carew, Rt Hon. W.H. Ford Cogan, W. Colles, Baron de Robeck (Fock), J. Doherty, C.J. Engledow, C.W. FitzGerald, Rt Hon. Lord O.A. FitzGerald (later treasurer and Comptroller of the Household), W. Fletcher, A.W. Harris, Sir J. W. Hart, Sir E. Kennedy, P.J. Kennedy, D. Kilbride, A.G. Lefroy, N.P. Leader, J. Leahy, C.H. Meldon, M.J. Minch, Capt H.F. Morgan, D. O'Connor Henchy, J. O'Connor, Rt Hon. R. More O'Farrell, J.A. O'Neill, W. Reade, C. Roberts, E. Ruthven, W. Talbot and R. Williams.

2. CIVIL WAR CASUALTIES

Pro-treaty casualties included (1922 unless stated): Pte Patrick Allison, Graney, KIA (no date). Pte Joe Bergen discovered dead at Milltown, near Newbridge on 16 August 1923. Pte Edward Byrne, Graney, KIA 24 October. Pte Patrick Donoghoe, a dispatch rider who was wounded when ambushed at an unspecified location on 19 July died from his wounds at the Curragh Hospital on 19 September 1923. Pte James Hunt from WIA at Graney, 24 December. Pte Patrick Lynch from WIA, died Curragh Hospital 12 January 1923. Pte Thomas

McEvoy, Graney, died 1 January 1923. Pte Joseph Moran KIA Leixlip, 1 December. Pte James Murray KIA Castledermot, 24 November. Sgt Edward O'Neill died in Naas County Home on 20 August from gunshot wounds.

Anti-Treaty casualties included (all 1922 unless stated): R. Monks (30 August) while imprisoned in the Curragh. Sylvester Sheppard and Laurence Sweeney, KIA in Castledermot on 5 July. Four men from Kildare town—Patrick Bagnall and Patrick Mangan from Fairgreen, Joseph Johnston from Station Road and Stephen White from Abbey Street—were tried by committee with Brian Moore and Patrick Nolan from Rathbride and were executed in Dublin on 19 December. Thomas Dunne from Castledermot died GSW on 16 June. R. Monks died in custody in the Curragh Camp on 30 August, while a man named Gleeson died there on 26 January 1923. At Newbridge Camp, Denis Barry died on 20 January after a hunger strike, while Owen Boyle died in custody on 13 November.

During 1923, after the cease-fire, a number of deaths occurred. In the Curragh they were: Joseph Bergin of Milltown Bridge on 15 December; Daniel Downey on 10 June of ill-health due to imprisonment and hunger strike; Joe Whitty on 2 September, Dick Humes on 9 November and Joseph Lacey on 24 December after a hunger strike; and Frank O'Keefe (date unknown).

3. DEPUTIES ELECTED TO DÁIL ÉIREANN

(See Glossary for explanation of abbreviations)

KILDARE AND WICKLOW

1922   Christopher M. Byrne (CT), Hugh Colohan and James Everett (Lab), Richard Wilson (F) and Robert Childers Barton (CR)

KILDARE

1923   H.J. Colohan (Lab), J. Conlan (Farmers), G. Wolfe (C na nG)
1927   (June and September) G. Wolfe (C na nG), D. Buckley (FF), H. Colohan (Lab)
1931   By-Election due to death of H. Colohan. T. Harris (FF)
1932   T. Harris (FF), W. Norton (Lab), Capt S.B.Minch (C na nG)
1933   T. Harris (FF), W. Norton (Lab), Capt S.B. Minch (C na nG, later FG)

CARLOW-KILDARE

1937   W. Norton (Lab), S. Minch (FG), T. Harris (FF), F. Humphreys (Carlow, FF)
1938   T Harris (FF), W. Norton (Lab), J. Hughes (Carlow, FG), F. Humphreys (FF)
1943   W. Norton (Lab), T. Harris (FF), J. Hughes (FG), Dr T. Humphreys (FF)
1944   T. Harris (FF), J. Hughes (FG), W. Norton, F. Humphreys (Carlow, FF)

CO. KILDARE

1948   T. Harris (FF), W. Norton (Lab), G. Sweetman (FG)
1951   T. Harris (FF), W. Norton (Lab), G. Sweetman (FG)
1954   W. Norton (Lab), G. Sweetman (FG), T. Harris (FF)
1957   W. Norton (Lab), P. Dooley (FF), G. Sweetman (FG)
1961   W. Norton (Lab), G. Sweetman (FG), P. Dooley (FF), B. Crinion (FF)
1964   By-Election due to W. Norton's death. T. Boylan (FF)
1965   B. Crinion (FF), P. Norton (Lab), G. Sweetman (FG), T. Boylan (FF)
1969   T. Boylan (FF), G. Sweetman (FG), P. Power (FF)
1970   By-Election due to death of G. Sweetman in a motor-car accident)
       P. Malone (FG)
1973   P. Power (FF), J. Bermingham (Lab), P. Malone (FG)
1977   P. Power (FF), J. Bermingham (Lab), C. McCreevy (FF)
1981   P. Power (FF), C. McCreevy (FF), J. Bermingham (Lab), B. Durkan (FG), A.
       Dukes (FG)
February 1982 C. McCreevy (FF), A. Dukes (FG), J. Bermingham (Lab), P. Power
       (FF), G. Brady (FF)
November 1982 B. Durkan (FG), C. McCreevy (FF), A. Dukes (FG), P. Power (FF),
       J. Bermingham (Lab)
1987   P. Power (FF), E. Stagg (Lab), A. Dukes (FG), B. Durkan (FG), C. McCreevy
       (FF)
1989   A. Dukes (FG), C. McCreevy (FF), E. Stagg (Lab), B. Durkan (FG), S. Power
       (FF)
1992   E. Stagg (Lab), C. McCreevy (FF), A. Dukes (FG), S. Power (FF), B. Durkan
       (FG)

KILDARE NORTH

1997   B. Durkan (FG), C. McCreevy (FF), E. Stagg (Lab)
2002   C. McCreevy (FF), E. Stagg (Lab), B. Durkan (FG)

KILDARE SOUTH

1997   A. Dukes (FG), S. Power (FF), J. Wall (Lab)
2002   S. Power (FF), S. Ó Fearghail (FF), J. Wall (Lab)

4. KILDARE COUNTY COUNCIL CHAIRMEN

The position of Co. Council Chairman has been filled by: Stephen J. Brown
(1899–1910), Matthew Minch (1911–19), Dómhnall Ó Buachalla (1920–22),
Michael Fitzsimons (1923–33), Thomas Harris (1934–41), Michael Smyth
(1942–44), Thomas Harris (1945–48), Gerard Sweetman (1949–50), Michael
Smyth (1951), Gerard Sweetman (1952), Michael Smyth (1953), A.W. Moore

(1954), Thomas Carbery (1955), A.W. Moore (1956), Michael Cunningham (1957–58), James Dowling (1959), Michael Cunningham (1960), Terence Boylan (1961–62), Michael St. Ledger (1963), Michael Cunningham (1964), Terence Boylan (1965), James Dowling (1966), Michael Cunningham (1967), Terence Boylan (1968), James Dowling (1969), Michael St. Ledger (1970), Michael Cunningham (1971), Andrew Mahon (1972), Michael Brady (1973), John McKenna (1974), Terence Boylan (1975), John O'Neill (1976), Michael McWey (1977), Austin Groome (1978), Michael McWey (1979), Joseph Bermingham (1980), Patrick Hyland (1981), Emmet Stagg (1982), Patricia Lawlor (1983), James O'Loughlin (1984), Timothy Conway (1985), Bernard Durkan (1986), Gerry Brady (1987), Michael McWey (1988), James O'Loughlin (1989), James Gallagher (1990), James O'Loughlin (1991), Michael McWey (1992), John O'Neill (1993), Michael Nolan (1994), Sean Ó Feargháil (1995), Sean Reilly (1996), Liam Doyle (1997), Jim Reilly (1998), P.J. Sheridan (1999), Rainsford Hendy (2000) and John O'Neill (2001–02). Councillors agreed on Monday 10 June 2002 that the county's premier citizen should carry the title Mayor of the County of Kildare. John O'Neill was the first holder of the title.

NOTES

NOTE TO CHAPTER 2 (pp 3–9)

1. Kinahan, G. Henry, *Geology of Ireland*, London 1878.

NOTES TO CHAPTER 3 (pp 10–20)

1. *Lives of Saints from the Book of Lismore*, Ed. Trans. Stokes, W., Oxford 1890.
2. *Patrologica Latina*, Athens 1879.

NOTES TO CHAPTER 4 (pp 21–38)

1. *The Annals of the Four Masters*, trans. O'Donovan, John, 6 vols., Dublin 1848–67. (See Annals, Glossary.)
2. *Topographia Hiberniae [The History and Topography of Ireland]* trans. O'Meara, J., Mountrath 1951.
3. Cambro-Norman settlers often named the places they received in grant and added 'town' to their own name. For example, Co. Kildare had Arthurstown, Bodenstown, Harristown, Sherlockstown, Osberstown, Painstown and Kerdiffstown (recalling Cardiff). They also named after features, e.g. Loughtown, Milltown. Some used names of their Welsh places of origin

that still exist or that appear in old legal deeds from the Gower Peninsula, Glamorganshire and Pembrokeshire; names like Castlemartin, Newcastle, Whitechurch, Hodgestown, Colbinstown, Robertstown, Halverstown and others.

4. *Foras Feasa ar Éirinn* (Lit.: Foundation of Knowledge of Ireland, i.e. 5. History of Ireland, written 1629–31), Vol. 1 trans., Comyn, D., 1902.

5. *JCKAS Vol.* III, No. 5, p. 336.

NOTES TO CHAPTER 5 (pp 39–52)

1. Up to 1542, Co. Meath included the present Co. Westmeath.
2. National MSS XLI quoted in Gilbert, John, *Viceroys of Ireland,* Dublin 1865.
3. Edited from old English version cited in de Burgh, Thomas, 'Ancient Naas', *JCKAS* Vol. I, No. 3.
4. An Irish Manuscripts Commission edition bears the title *The Red Book of the Earls of Kildare* and a photocopied version of the original is held in the National Library of Ireland.
5. It took place in Christ Church and tradition tells that the crown used was taken from a statue of the Blessed Virgin Mary in nearby Saint Mary's Church.
6. Cited without source reference in de Burgh, Thomas, 'Ancient Naas', *JCKAS* Vol. I, No. 3.
7. Trinity College Library. MSS. No. 1. Edited from its reproduction contained in Appendix A, Mac Lysaght, *Irish Life in the Seventeenth Century,* Cork 1950.
8. Snoddy, Oliver, 'The Volunteers, Militia, Yeomanry and Orangemen of Co. Kildare in the Eighteenth Century', *JCKAS* Vol. XV, No. I.

NOTES TO CHAPTER 6 (pp 53–79)

1. The Rebellion Papers (620/37/176), National Archives.
2. O'Farrell, Padraic, ed., *The '98 Reader,* Dublin 1998.
3. The Rebellion Papers (620/37/211), National Archives.
4. Mac Suibhne, Peadar, *Kildare in '98,* Naas 1978.
5. *Recitations, Monologues, Character Sketches and Plays by Val Vousden,* Dublin (undated).
6. O'Farrell, Padraic, ed., *The '98 Reader,* Dublin 1998.
7. The Rebellion Papers (620/38/73), National Archives.
8. Musgrave, who gives an appalling account of the incident, says (p.252) that Doorley 'approached him with a menacing aspect and flourished a scimitar over his head, using at the same time some insolent and opprobious language.'

9. O'Brien, R. Barry, ed., *The Autobiography of Theobald Wolfe Tone*, Dublin (undated).

NOTES TO CHAPTER 7 (pp 80–126)

1. Delaney, Ruth, *Ireland's Inland Waterways*, Belfast 1988, p. 101.
2. Royal Canal Company Minutes, Vol. 4. 10 June 1824, quoted in Delaney, Ruth, *Ireland's Royal Canal*, Dublin 1992.
3. Quoted in Guinness, Desmond, *The Irish House*, Dublin 1975. Jonathan Swift (1667–1745) also wrote in 'A Letter to the Tradesmen Shop-Keepers, Farmers and Country-People in General in the Kingdom of Ireland': They say SQUIRE CONOLLY has Sixteen Thousand Pounds a year; now if he sends for his Rent to Town, as it is likely he does, he must have Two Hundred and Fifty Horses to bring up his Half-Year's Rent and Two or Three great Cellars in his House for Stowage.
4. Census Returns. National Archives.
5. Outrage Papers 13/145. National Archives. Quoted in paper by Comerford, R.V. 'Co. Kildare and the Famine'
6. Quoted in *Rebel Worker,*1 June 1998.
7. *JCKAS* Vol. VII, No. 6, p. 413.
8. Mac Giolla Choille, Breandán (ed.), *Intelligence Notes from the Chief Secretary's Office, Dublin Castle from 1913–16*, Dublin 1966.
9. Ibid.
10. Military Archives, Box 8, Civil War Operations, Dublin Command. Civil War Courtmartial.
11. Kildare County Council Minute Book, April 1899, quoted in Kenny, Liam, *Kildare Council 1899–1999*, Naas 1999.
12. Quoted in O'Farrell, Padraic, *By Rail Through the Heart of Ireland*, Dublin & Cork 1990.
13. O'Connor, Pat, Pamphlet, NLI P2070.
14. *Annual Housing Statistics Bulletin 2001*, Department of the Environment and Local Government.

BIBLIOGRAPHY

PRIMARY SOURCES

Author's notes for proposed memoir of youth in Co. Kildare.
Carey family (Donadea) personal notes (1850–1936).
Census Returns, NLI.
Certification and correspondence held at Archives North America, Loretto Abbey, 101 Mason Boulevard, Toronto.
Church of Ireland records.
Civil Defence School documents and correspondence.
Correspondence from the Office of the Governor General. NLI.
Devon Commission, 1 Oct 01, NLI.
Famine Relief Commission documents, NLI.
Intelligence Reports, 1922. Military Archives.
Leinster Papers, NLI.
Lyons, Mary Ann, 'Church and Society in Early Sixteenth Century Kildare', MA Thesis, Russell Library, Maynooth, 1991.
MSS of research by Lena Boylan, Trustee of Castletown House, Co. Kildare.
Meath & Kildare Dioceses records.
National School Manuscript Sources, Co. Kildare.
Department of Irish Folklore, University College, Dublin.
Ó hÓgáin, Dáithí. Letter to Minister for the Environment outlining importance of Hill of Allen.
Office of Public Works documents, plans and correspondence.
Outrage Papers, NAI.

Private Secretary's correspondence, NAI.
Rebellion papers, NAI
Records of Commissioners of Education, NAI
Register of Kilmainham Jail, NAI
State of the Country papers, NAI.

REFERENCE WORKS, UNPUBLISHED WORKS, JOURNALS AND DOCUMENTS

All the Year Round, 26 November 1864.
Annual Housing Statistics Bulletin 2001, Department of the Environment and Local Government.
Annual Registers, NLI.
Athy Heritage Company literature.
Bord na Móna, Vol 7, No 1, Spring 1959.
Boylan, Henry, *A Dictionary of Irish Biography* (Second Edition), Dublin 1988.
Brady, Anne M. & Cleeve, Brian, *A Biographical Dictionary of Irish Writers*, Mullingar 1985.
Burke's Landed Gentry in Ireland (assorted editions).
Burke's Peerage (assorted editions).
Burne, Jerome, (ed.) *Chronicle of the World*, (London 1989).
Capuchin Annual, 1970.
Census of Ireland. General Alphabetical Index to Townlands and Towns, Parishes and Baronies of Ireland, Dublin 1861.
Comerford, R.V., 'Co. Kildare and the Famine' paper in *Lest We Forget*–Naas (undated).
Co. Kildare Fáilte Ltd., Information packs, booklets and brochures.
Cullen, Mary, *Maynooth–Magh Nuad* (Private, undated).
Cummins, Seamus, *A Shout in the Night–The Rise and Fall of the Leixlip Irregulars July-December 1922.*
Devon Commission on Land in Ireland, 1845 (Vols I to III), NLI.
Devon Commission on Land in Ireland, Evidence of Commissioners of Inquiry, Three Vols. Thom, Dublin 1845.
Eason's Irish Heritage Series, Vols. 49, 51, 69.
Greshaw's Magazine, March 1787.
Hanmer's Chronicle.
Hogan, Robert, *Dictionary of Irish Literature*, Vols I and II, London 1996.
Irish Independent (Author's contributions).
Journals of Co. Kildare Archaeological Society (JCKAS).
Kenny, Liam, *Kildare Council 1899–1999*, Naas 1999.
Kildare and the Great Famine, Naas (undated).
Kildare Co. Council, *Lest We Forget* (undated).
Kildare Fáilte, information packs, booklets and brochures.
Leinster Leader.
Lewis, Samuel, *Topographical Dictionary of Ireland*, Vol I. 1837.

Maynooth Research Guides to Irish Local History.

Midland-East Tourism, information packs, booklets and brochures.

Mullins, Brian, 'Fianna Fáil in Co. Kildare from 1927–1937', Maynooth, 1999.

Naas Local History Group, *Nás na Riogh– From Poorhouse Road to The Fairy Flax*, Naas (undated).

O'Connor, Pat, Pamphlet, NLI, P2070.

O'Donovan, John, ed/trs., *Annals of the Kingdom of Ireland*, Vols. I to 7. Dublin 1849–51 (*Annals of the Four Masters*).

O'Donovan, John, *Ordnance Survey Letters*.

Oughterany. Journal of the Donadea Local History Group, Vols. I to IV.

Pall Mall Gazette, 1867.

Paper on Hill of Allen by VOICE environmental organisation.

Parliamentary Gazetteer of Ireland (The), Dublin 1844/5, London & Edinburgh 1846.

Porter's Post Office Guide .

Telford, S., *Athy*.

The Irish Builder, Vol XXXV, No. 804.

The Irish Defence Forces—A Handbook, (ed.) Pender, A, Dublin 1988.

The Irish Printer, Vol XXXV, No. 804.

The Irish Times (Author's contributions).

Thom's Irish Almanac and Official Directory (assorted editions).

INTERNET AND CD ROMS

ElectionsIreland.org.

Encarta World Atlas CD.

Encyclopaedia Brittanica De Luxe Millennium Edition CD.

Index to Griffith's Valuation of Ireland 1848–64 CD.

Ireland.com.

JCKAS Index.

Kildare.ie.

Penguin Hutchinson Reference Suite CD.

PRONI sites.

Rebel Worker. Irish Anarcho-Syndicalist monthly home page.

Rootsweb.com.

BOOKS

Allen, Gregory, *The Garda Síochána*, Dublin 1999.

A Loreto Sister, *Joyful Mother of Children: Mother Frances Mary Teresa Ball*, Dublin 1961.

Andrews, C.S., *Some Precursors of Bord na Móna*, Dublin 1954.

Andrews, J.H., *Irish Historic Towns Atlas No. 1 Kildare*, Dublin 1986.

Barry, Rev. A., *Lives of the Irish Saints*, Dublin (undated).

Bartlett, Thomas, (ed.) *Life of Theobald Wolfe Tone*, Dublin 1998.

Berleth, Richard, *The Twilight Lords*, London 1979.

Berresford Ellis, Peter, *A Dictionary of Irish Mythology*, Oxford 1987.

Bodkin, M. McDonnell, *Lord Edward FitzGerald*, Dublin (undated).

Brabazon, Aubrey, *Racing Through My Mind*, Waterford 1998.

Bradley, Bruce, *James Joyce's Schooldays*, Dublin 1982.

Breathnach, Diarmuid, *Almanag Éireannach*, Baile Átha Cliath 1981.

Browne, Vincent, (ed.) *Magill Book of Politics*, Dublin 1981.

Brynn, Edward, *Crown & Castle*, Dublin 1978.

Byrne, Liam, *History of Aviation In Ireland*, Dublin 1980.

Carville, Geraldine, *Monasterevin and Its People*, Monasterevin:Dublin 1999.

Chambers, Liam, *Rebellion in Kildare 1790–1803*, Dublin 1998.

Coill Dubh Book Committee, *Coill Dubh*, Coill Dubh 1993.

Comerford, M., *Collections Relating to the Dioceses of Kildare and Leighlin*, Dublin 1883.

Comerford, R.V., *The Fenians in Context*, Dublin 1985.

Conlan, Patrick, *Franciscan Ireland*, Mullingar 1988.

Conlon/deCourcy, *Anna Liffey*, Dublin 1988.

Connolly, Mary, *From Connell to Droichead Nua*, Naas:Newbridge 2001.

Connolly, S.J., (ed.) *The Oxford Companion to Irish History*, Oxford 2002.

Conyngham, D.P., *Lives of The Irish Saints*, New York/Philadelphia (undated)

Corish, Patrick J., *The Catholic Community*, Dublin 1981.

Corrigan, Mario, *All that Delirium of the Brave*, Naas 1987.

Cosgrove, Art, *Late Medieval Ireland*, 1370–1541, Dublin 1981.

Costello, Con., *A Most Delightful Station*, Cork 1996.

Costello, Con., *Guide to Kildare & Wicklow*, Naas 1991.

Costello, Peter, *Clongowes Wood—A History of Clongowes Wood College*, Dublin 1989.

Craig, Maurice & The Knight of Glin, *Ireland Observed*, Dublin:Cork 1970.

Crealey, Aidan H., *An Irish Almanac*, Dublin:Cork 1993.

Crystal, David, (ed.) *The Cambridge Biographical Encyclopedia*, Cambridge 1994.

Cullen/Geissel, (eds.) *Fugitive Warfare—1798 in North Kildare*, Clane 1998.

Darvill, Timothy, *The Concise Oxford Dictionary of Archaeology*, Oxford 2002.

De Blacam, Hugh, *The Saints of Ireland*, U.S.A. 1942.

Delaney, Ruth, *Grand Canal of Ireland*, Newtown Abbott 1972.

Delaney, Ruth, *Ireland's Inland Waterways*, Belfast 1988.

Delaney, Ruth, *Ireland's Royal Canal*, Dublin 1992.

Delany, V.T.H. & D.R. *The Canals of the South of Ireland*, Newtown Abbot 1966.

Dickson, David, Keogh, Dáire & Whelan, Kevin, (ed.) *The United Irishmen*, Dublin 1993.

Douglas/Harte/O'Hara, *Ireland Since 1690*, Belfast 1999.

Duffy, Seán, *Ireland in the Middle Ages*, Dublin 1997.

Dunny, Patrick, (ed.) *Prosperous—A Village of Vision*, (undated).

Ellis, S.G., *Tudor Ireland: Crown Community and Conflict of Cultures 1470–1603*, London 1985.

Faly, Patrick C., (ed.) *Ninety Eight: being the recollections of Cormac Cahir O'Conor Faly*, London 1897.

Feehan, John, & O'Donovan, Grace, *The Bogs of Ireland*, Dublin 1996.

Feehan, John, *The Landscape of Slieve Bloom*, Dublin 1979.

Fitz-Simon. Christopher, *The Arts in Ireland—A Chronology*, Dublin 1982.

Flanagan, Deirdre & Laurence, *Irish Place Names*, Dublin 1994.

Frame, Robin, *Colonial Ireland, 1169–1369*, Dublin 1981.

Gibson, W.H., *Early Irish Golf*, Two-Mile-House, Naas 1988.

Guinness, Desmond, *The Irish House*, Dublin 1975.

Hayes-McCoy, G.A., *Irish Battles*, Dublin 1980.

Hickey, D.J. & Doherty, J.E., *A Chronology of Irish History Since 1500*, Dublin 1989.

Hickey, D.J. & Doherty, J.E., *A Dictionary of Irish History 1800–1980*, Dublin 1980.

Hopkinson, Michael, *Green Against Green*, Dublin 1988.

Houghton, Raymond W., Berman, David, & Lapan, Maureen T., *Images of Berkeley*, Dublin 1986.

Joyce, P. W., *A Short History of Ireland*, London 1904.

Joyce, P. W., *A Social History of Ancient Ireland*, (Vols I and II), Dublin 1920.

Joyce, P. W., *A Social History of Ancient Ireland*, (Vol II), Dublin 1903.

Joyce, P. W., *The Origin and History of Irish Names of Places* (Vols I to III), Dublin, 1893–1913.

Kavanagh, Michael V., *A Bibliography of the History of Co. Kildare*, Droichead Nua 1976.

Kee, Robert, *Ireland—A History*, London 1980.

Kerryman Ltd, *With The I.R.A. In The Fight For Freedom*, Tralee (undated).

Killanin, Lord & Duignan, Michael V., *The Shell Guide To Ireland*, Dublin 1962.

Killen, John, (ed.) *The Decade of the United Irishmen*, Belfast 1997.

Kinahan, G. Henry, *Geology of Ireland*, London 1878.

Kinealy, Christine, *This Great Calamity The Irish Famine 1845–1852*, Dublin 1994.

Leadbeater, Mary, *Memoirs and Letters of Richard & Elizabeth Shackleton*, London 1849.

Ledwith, Mícheál, *Maynooth College*, Maynooth 1984.

Longford, Lord (Frank Pakenham), *Peace By Ordeal*, London 1935.

Lyons, F.S.L., *Ireland Since the Famine* (Revised), London 1973.

Macalister, R.A.S., *The Archaeology of Ireland*, London 1928.

Madden, R.R., *The United Irishmen, their Lives and Times*, Vols I to VII. Dublin 1842–1846.

McEvoy, John, *Carlow College 1793–1993* (undated).

Mac Giolla Choille, Breandán, (ed.) *Intelligence Notes from the Chief Secretary's Office, Dublin Castle from 1913–1916*, Dublin 1966.

Mc Govern, Kathleen I.B.V.M., *Something More than Ordinary*, Toronto (undated).

MacLysaght, Edward, *Irish Families*, Dublin 1957.

MacLysaght, Edward, *The Surnames of Ireland*, Dublin 1978.

MacLysaght, E., *Irish Life in the Seventeenth Century*, Cork:Oxford 1920.

Mac Suibhne, Peadar, *Kildare In '98*, Naas 1978.

Magee, Malachy, *1000 Years of Irish Whiskey*, Dublin 1980.

Maher, Mary, *Footsteps of Irish Saints*, London 1927.

Mahon-Behan, Vera, *Athy and District*, (undated).

Manning, Maurice, *The Blueshirts*, Dublin 1971.

Martin, F.X., *The Irish Volunteers 1913–1915*, Dublin 1963.

Maxwell, Constantia, *The Stranger in Ireland*, Dublin 1979.

McKee, Michael, *Conflict and Curses in Carbury*, Newbridge 1997.

McLoughlin, Mark, (ed.) *The Curragh–A Lifetime of Memories*, Curragh 1997.

McMahon, Sean, *Irish Placenames*, Dublin 1990.

Moody, T.W. & Martin, F.X., *The Course of Irish History*, Cork 1984.

Moody, T.W., Martin, F.X. & Byrne, F.J., *A New History of Ireland Vols I to X*, Oxford 1976.

Moore, Des, *Off-Beat Ireland*, Dublin (undated).

Musgrave, Richard, *Sir Richard Musgrave's Memoirs of the Different Rebellions in Ireland*, Dublin 1801.

Nelson, G., *A History of Leixlip, Co. Kildare*, 1990.

Nelson, T., *The Land War in Co. Kildare*, Dublin (undated).

Newman, Roger Chatterton, *Brian Boru*, Dublin 1983.

O'Brien, R. Barry, (ed) *The Autobiography of Theobald Wolfe Tone*, Dublin (undated).

O'Connor, Catherine, (ed) *Cutover & Cutaway Bogs*, Dublin 2000.

O'Connor, Dermod, (ed.) *Keating's General History of Ireland*, Dublin (undated).

O'Connor, Frank, *Leinster, Munster & Connaught*, London (undated).

O'Farrell, Padraic, *By Rail Through the Heart of Ireland*, Dublin:Cork 1990.

O'Farrell, Padraic, *Down Ratra Road*, Dublin 2000.

O'Farrell, Padraic, *Irish Rogues, Rascals and Scoundrels*, Dublin 1992.

O'Farrell, Padraic, *Irish Saints*, Dublin 2002.

O'Farrell, Padraic, *Irish Surnames*, Dublin 2002.

O'Farrell, Padraic, *Tell Me Sean O'Farrell*, Dublin:Cork 1986.

O'Farrell, Padraic, (ed.) *The '98 Reader*, Dublin 1998.

O'Farrell, Padraic, *Who's Who In The Irish War Of Independence And Civil War 1916–23*, Dublin 1977.

O'Hanlon, John, *Lives of the Irish Saints*, Dublin 1862.

O'Sullivan, T. F., *Goodly Barrow*, Dublin 1983.

Pakenham, Thomas, *The Year of Liberty*, London 1969.

Palmer, A.W., *The Penguin Dictionary of Modern History*, Middlesex 1973.

Palmer, A.W., *The Penguin Dictionary of Twentieth Century History 1900–1978*, Middlesex 1979.

Paterson, John, *Meath & Kildare- An Historical Guide*, Kingscourt 1981.

Póirtéir, Cathal, (ed.) *The Great Irish Rebellion of 1798*, Dublin:Cork 1998.

Popplewell, Seán, (ed.) *The Irish Museums Guide*, Dublin 1983.

Powell, T.G.E., *The Celts*, London 1958.

Roche, Richard, *The Norman Invasion of Ireland*, Dublin 1979.

Shackleton, Sir Ernest, *South*, London 1999.

Sheehy, Maurice, *When The Normans Came To Ireland*, Dublin 1975.

Shiel, Michael, *The Quiet Revolution*, Dublin 1984.

Spenser, E., *A View of the Present State of Ireland*, Dublin 1763.

Stokes, Whitely, (ed.) *Lives of the Saints from the Book of Lismore*, Oxford 1890.

Stravinskas, Peter M.J., *Catholic Encyclopedia*, Indiana 1991.

Taaffe, Pat, *Eye on Athy's Past*, Athy 2000.

Tillyard, Stella, *Citizen Lord Edward FitzGerald 1763–1798*, London 1997.

Walker, Brian E., *Parliamentary Election Results in Ireland 1801–1922*, Dublin 1978.

Weir, Anthony, *Early Ireland*, Belfast 1980.

Williams, E.N., *The Penguin Dictionary of English And European History*, Middlesex 1980.

GLOSSARY

AD	*Anno Domini.* In the year of the Lord. Of the Christian period.
Abhainn Life	Avon Liffey. Anna Livia. Liffey.
Act of Union	The British and Irish parliaments passed two similar measures in 1800 to create the United Kingdom of Great Britain and Ireland. The resulting Act of Union came into force on 1 January 1801.
Aidhne	See Uí Fiachrach, below.
Aileach	The territory that, in the main, is now Co. Donegal. 'The Grianán of Aileach', the Northern Uí Néill seat, was a fortified site on Greenan Mountain in Donegal. Muiriertach O'Brien, King of Munster, destroyed it in 1101 in revenge for the destruction of Kincora of the Munster kings.
Ailinn	Beautiful (Knockaulin Cnoc Ailinn. Beautiful Hill).
Almhuin	Allen.
annals	A number of Annals chronicle Irish affairs over certain periods. Those referred to are *Innisfallen* (eleventh to fourteenth centuries), *The Four Masters (Annales Rioghachta Éireann)* Annals of the Kingdom of Ireland. (1632–36), *Tighernach* (late eleventh century, but this is disputed), *Loch Cé* (1014–1590), *Connaught (Annála Connacht)* (1224–1554) and *Ulster* (fifteenth to seventeenth centuries).
Ballybetagh	Lit. *baile biataigh*, home of a public hospitaller. Medieval subdivision of a cantred (see below).
Ballyboe	Another name for ballybetagh, above.
Bann Flake	Bann Culture is a general name for the late Mesolithic flint industries of Northern Ireland and the Isle of Man.

They were part of more widely distributed Late Mesolithic cultures. In Ireland, they dated to between 5500 BC and 3800 BC. Leaf-shaped flakes or Bann Flakes appeared in characteristic heavy blades.

barony
A sub-division of a county.

Battle of Benburb
In Co. Tyrone, on 5 June 1646, Owen Roe O'Neill (Confederate Catholics) beat the Scottish forces under Munro who were defending the Ulster planters.

Battle of Kinsale
24 December 1601. A Spanish Expeditionary Force landed but was contained by Lord Mountjoy. Mountjoy then routed Hugh O'Neill (Earl of Tyrone) and Red Hugh O'Donnell who had marched south to assist the Spanish. The Spanish then withdrew.

bawn
(*bábhún*/Walled enclosure). A defensive courtyard built by landlords owning over 1,000 acres. In farming, a paddock close to farmhouses (from *bán*. Grassland. Lea)

BC
Before Christ

Bealtaine
(*Béal Tine*/Mouth of Fire) 1 May. One of the four great pre-Christian festivals. The others were Samhain (31 October), Imbolg (1 February) and Lughnasa (also Lammas, an agrarian festival held in August).

bóithrín
(Small road) Narrow lane or road.

Book of Armagh
Contains the *Confessions* of St Patrick, a copy of the New Testament, lives of saints including Saint Martin of Tours, all compiled by Feardomhnach the Scribe c. 807.

Bóramha
(or Boremeau) Tribute paid in cattle. The cow (bó) was a pre-Christian unit of value.

Breffny
The territory that is now Co. Cavan, Co. Leitrim and parts of counties Sligo and Fermanagh. Also Breifne, Breiffiny, Breifny and Breny.

Brehon Law or System
The legal system that existed prior to the Anglo-Norman Invasion. *Breitheamh* means judge.

Brian Ború
(c. 941–1014) 'Brian of the [Cattle]Tributes' was so called because of his exacting them from the O'Neills. He was King of Dál gCais (see below) and later High King of Ireland. He is renowned for defeating the Leinster men and their Norse allies at the Battle of Clontarf (Dublin) in 1014 before being killed by a fleeing enemy.

Calp
Originally Black Carboniferous limestone, later adapted to denote one of the lithological divisions of Carboniferous rocks.

Cambro-Normans
Normans (q.v.) who settled in Wales. Also called Cumbro-Normans.

cantred
An Anglo-Norman term for a political division that existed before their conquest. It often coincided with the boundaries of a deanery.

C.C.	Catholic curate.
Cenél Eacgrach	An Ulster population group.
Cenél Eoghan	Tyrone and Derry descendants of Eoghan, a son of Niall of the Nine Hostages (see below) i.e. O'Neills.
cineál	Race or descendants.
clan	A Scottish group with common ancestors, particularly Highlanders under patriarchal control. There was no Irish clan system.
C na nG	Cumann na nGaedhal. A political designation.
co-arb	See *erenagh*, below.
cognate	Descended from a common ancestor.
Córas Iompair Éireann	Transport Company of Ireland (CIÉ).
Corn Laws	Regulations existed from the twelfth century controlling imports and exports of grain. Landowners who wished to maintain high domestic corn prices were prominent in government in 1815 and they incorporated the regulations into a Corn Law. An Anti-Corn Law League emerged and received the backing of Sir Robert Peel (1788–1850) who repealed it in 1846 but was forced to resign as Prime Minister.
coyne and livery	From the Irish *coinmheadh* (billeting) and the English livery (free food and clothing for retainers in a household). The phrase indicated free board, lodgings and often a wage given by lords to galloglass (see below), kern and assorted employees.
CR	Coalition Republic. A political designation.
'Crom Abú'	The FitzGerald war cry. 'Croom [castle, Co. Limerick], to victory'.
CT	Coalition Treaty. A political designation.
cúige	Province (a fifth).
Cumann na mBan	(Women's Association) A women's organisation founded in 1913 that became a division of the Irish Volunteers.
Cumbro-Normans	See Cambro-Normans, above.
Dáil Éireann	The Irish parliament, commonly referred to as the Dáil.
dál	Region.
Dalcassians	See Dál gCais below.
Decies	A region in the west of the present Co. Waterford.
Desmond	South Munster territory that included the present Co. Kerry and much of Co. Cork (See Eoghanacht, below).
Diarmuid MacMurrough	(Mac Murchadha) (1110–1171) A King of Leinster who was the primary cause of the Anglo-Norman Invasion.
DMP	Dublin Metropolitan Police.
donn	Brown.
EEC	European Economic Community.

Eoghanacht	In the third century, a Munster King, Oilioll Olum, had sons Eoghan and Cormac Cas. When he died, Cormac Cas inherited Thomond. (See below and Dalcassian, above). Eoghan received the territory of Desmond (see above). His family were known as the Eoghanacht.
eponymous ancestor	The person from whom a family name originated.
erenagh	The *aircinnech* (erenagh) or lay head of a church. Church property was handed down to his family. An ordained head or abbot was called co-arb (comarba: heir).
ESB	Electricity Supply Board.
F	Farmers' Union. A political designation.
fairche	Parish.
FBI	Federal Bureau of Investigation (USA).
Fenians	A republican movement founded formally during 1858 by James Stephens in Dublin and John O'Mahoney in New York.
FF	Fianna Fáil, Irish political party.
FG	Fine Gael, Irish political party.
Fionn	Fair.
'Flight of the Earls'	A romantic term for the self-imposed exile in 1607 of Rory O'Donnell, Earl of Tirchonaill, Hugh O'Neill, Earl of Tyrone, Cúconnacht Maguire, Lord of Fermanagh, and their followers.
fl.	Flourished.
GAA	Gaelic Athletic Association (Cumann Luthcleas Gael).
Gaelic	(a) The language spoken in the Scottish highlands. (b) An adjective denoting the race inhabiting Ireland since the prehistoric era. (c) The language known in English as the Irish language now spelt Gaeilge in that tongue.
gallaun	A standing stone, often isolated.
galloglass	(*gall óglac*/foreign warrior. Sometimes gallowglass) Paid fighting man retained permanently as such by an Irish chieftain. The warriors were mainly from Innse Gall in the Hebrides (Scotland) and were heavily armed, while the kern (ceithearn/war band) were lightly armed.
GB	Great Britain.
Geraldine	(Gearaltach) A term used to describe the Fitzgerald family, medieval earls of Desmond and of Kildare. They and other English families were rebels who regarded themselves as gentlemen of blood and who became accomplices of the Irish. Members of the dynasty included The Earls of Desmond and of Kildare, Dukes of Leinster, Knights of Glin, White Knights and Knights of Kerry.
GSW	Gunshot wounds.

High King	The term describing pre-Norman rulers is confusing. Ard Rí, Rí Érenn, Rí Temro (king of Tara) and Rex Hiberniae were also used.
Home Rule	A concept whereby Ireland, Scotland and England would have a common sovereign, but each with its own executive at Westminster and a national council to bestow international statehood. A home parliament would handle domestic affairs.
Hy Many	See Uí Máine, below.
Iar Connacht	A region, mainly in west Connaught, now known as Connemara.
Iarthar Life	West Liffey.
Imbolg	See Bealtaine, above.
inlier	A geological term meaning the space occupied by one formation and completely surrounded by a later formation.
IRB	Irish Republican Brotherhood. A secret organisation founded in Dublin by James Stephens. Its funds came mainly from the Fenian (see above) movement.
Iregan	(Uí Riagáin) A region of ancient Ophaley now in the north-west Slieve Bloom Mountains of Co. Laois. The Ó Duinn (Dunne) ruled there. Anglicized also to Dooregan, Duoregan, Hyregan, Oregan, and Yregan.
Irish Volunteers	A southern nationalist force founded in November 1913.
ITGWU	Irish Transport and General Workers' Union.
JCKAS	Journal of County Kildare Archaeological Society.
Justiciar	More properly, 'Chief Justiciar'. The title given to the governor of Ireland from the late twelfth to the mid-fourteenth centuries. He was chief administrator, overall military commander and chief judge (see King's Lieutenant, below).
KIA	Killed in action.
King's Lieutenant	In late medieval times, this title was given to governors of Ireland who were of noble stock.
Kitchen midden	Normally coastal. Inland, as in Co. Kildare, a collection of axes, pins, arrow heads and the like found in ancient forts.
Lab	Labour Party, Irish political party.
Lammas	See Bealtaine, above.
Liberty	Anglo-Norman lordship exercising jurisdiction normally the Crown's prerogative. The king's writ sometimes ran but local lords were for the most part free from governmental interference.
Lieutenant	Titled Governors of Ireland sometimes used this nomenclature.
Lit	Literally.
Magh	Plain.

MEP	Member of the European Parliament.
MP	Member of Parliament.
NAI	National Archives of Ireland.
Nation, The	*The Irish Nation.* A journal founded in 1842 by Thomas Davis, John Blake Dillon and Sir Charles Gavan Duffy. First published in 1842, it espoused the establishment of 'internal union and external independence' and strove 'to create and foster public opinion and make it racy of the soil'. It developed into a voice for the Young Ireland movement.
NLI	National Library of Ireland.
Niall of the Nine Hostages	(Niall Noígiallach): Progenitor of the Uí Néill. Some sources place him as High King of Ireland from 379–405, others place his activities in the fifth and ninth centuries.
Nine Year War	(1593–1603). Also known as 'Tyrone's Rebellion' because the main protagonist was Hugh O'Neill, Second Earl of Tyrone. Elizabethan partition of Co. Monaghan sparked the conflict that split the MacMahon lordship. Traditional Ulster rivalry dissipated in face of the State's threat to lordships. The long campaign included celebrated battles like Clontibret (1595), the Yellow Ford (1598). The outcome, after O'Neill's submission at Mellifont in 1603, gave England complete control of Ireland for the first time since the Anglo-Norman invasion (see above).
NLI	National Library of Ireland.
O.F.M.	Order of Friars Minor.
Oirthear Life	East Liffey.
Oriel	(Orghialla). A region comprising the present counties of Monaghan and Armagh and parts of Down, Fermanagh and Louth.
Ossory	(Osraighe) A region comprising the present Co. Kilkenny and parts of adjoining counties.
Oughterany	An ancient name for a region in central north Kildare.
outlier	An artifact or site isolated from the main distribution of similar things or a standing stone removed from a stone circle.
Owney	Territory that later became incorporated in the Co. Tipperary barony of Owney and Arra.
paruchia	diocese.
pattern day	(Patron Day): A day of celebration, usually at a holy well of a patron saint.
Penal Laws	(or Popery Laws) Statutes introduced after 1695 discriminating against Roman Catholics.
PRONI	Public Records Office of Northern Ireland.
Quarter-day	A day on which quarterly tenancies began and on which rents and tithes became due.

rapparee	(Rapáire-half pike). A seventeenth century highwayman who sought to defend peasants from the oppressor or an independent, maverick soldier.
RC	Roman Catholic.
RE	Radio Éireann.
Red Branch Knights	Military guardians of Ulster during the reign of Conchubhar (Conor) Mac Nessa. Cuchullain was their renowned warrior.
Repealer	Anyone demanding repeal of the Act of Union (see above) and restoration of a separate Irish parliament.
RIC	Royal Irish Constabulary.
RTÉ	Radio Telefís Éireann. Ireland's national broadcasting service.
Samhain	See Bealtaine, above.
Seanchaí	(pl. *seanchíthe*) storyteller.
senchas	History.
sept	A collective term describing a group of people who bore a common surname and inhabited a particular area or whose ancestors were known to have occupied that area.
Seven Septs of Laois	Macaboys (i.e. MacEvoys. Also The Clandeboys), O'Devoys (or O'Deevys), O'Dorans, O'Dowlings, O'Kellys, O'Lalors, O'Mores.
SJ	Society of Jesus, better known as the Jesuits, a Roman Catholic religious order.
slean	A tool for cutting turf (peat).
SSI	Statistical Society of Ireland.
Tánaiste	Deputy Taoiseach (see below).
Taoiseach	(Leader, Ruler) The Prime Minister of the Government of Ireland.
TCD	Trinity College, Dublin. Dublin University.
TD	Teachta Dála: Deputy of Dáil Éireann (see above).
Thomond	*Tuath Mhumhan* or north Munster. A region taking in most of the present Co. Clare and portions of counties Tipperary and Limerick bordering it.
Tyrawley	A region in the present Co. Mayo.
Tírchonaill	(Land of Connell) A region covering the present Co. Donegal.
Tírowen	(Land of Eoghan) A region comprising the present Co. Tyrone and part of Derry.
toponymic	A surname that evolved from the name of a place.
trans.	Translated by.
Treaty, The	An agreement between Ireland and England signed on 6 December 1921 that gave independence to twenty-six counties of Ireland.

Tribes of Galway	Mainly Norman merchants controlling municipal administration. Some sources claim only seven but most recognise fourteen, viz: Athy, Blake, Bodkin, Browne, Darcy, Deane, Font, French, Joyce, Kirwan, Lynch, Martin, Morris and Skerret.
Tribes of Tara	(See Four Tribes of Tara, above).
Truce, The	Cessation of hostilities in the Irish War of Independence that came into effect on 11 July 1921.
tuam	Sepulchural mound.
tuath	(pl. tuatha) A petty kingdom or territory.
Tuatha Dé Danaan	(People of [the goddess] Dana). Pre-Christian gods.
UDC	Urban District Council.
Uí Ceathy	Ikeathy. An ancient name for a region in north Kildare.
Uí Drone	A population group of the present Co. Carlow.
Uí Fáilghe	(Uí Fáeláin, Uí Faoilain, Offelan) Co. Offaly. The baronies of East and West Offaly are in Co. Kildare.
Uí Máine	(or Hy Many) A population group in the centre of the present Co. Galway extending into the south of Co. Roscommon.
Uí Néill	See O'Neill, and Niall of the Nine Hostages, above.
UN	United Nations.
Union Flag	The flag of Great Britain and Ireland introduced in 1801 to incorporate Ireland.
WIA	Wounded in action.
Wild Geese	Irish chieftains, their soldiers and followers who fled to join foreign armies, mainly French, during the 18th century.
Young Irelanders	Followers of a nationalist movement led by Thomas Davis, Charles Gavan Duffy and John Blake Dillon (See *Nation, The*, above).
A hyphen between	dates denotes a period (e.g. Between the years 1222 and 1226 is given as 1222–26).

INDEX